STORYSELLING
for FINANCIAL ADVISORS

How Top Producers Sell

SCOTT WEST & MITCH ANTHONY

DEARBORN™
A **Kaplan Professional** Company

This publication is designed to provide accurate and authoritative information in regard to the subject matter covered. It is sold with the understanding that the publisher is not engaged in rendering legal, accounting, or other professional service. If legal advice or other expert assistance is required, the services of a competent professional should be sought.

Associate Publisher: Cynthia Zigmund
Managing Editor: Jack Kiburz
Project Editor: Trey Thoelcke
Interior Design: Lucy Jenkins
Cover Design: Scott Rattray, Rattray Design
Typesetting: the dotted i

Published by Dearborn
A Kaplan Professional Company

Printed in the United States of America

02 10 9 8 7 6 5

Library of Congress Cataloging-in-Publication Data

West, Scott, 1959–
    Storyselling for financial advisors: how top producers sell / Scott West, Mitch Anthony.
      p.   cm.
    Includes index.
    ISBN 0-7931-3664-4 (pbk.)
    1. Investment advisors—Marketing. 2. Selling—Psychological aspects. 3. Storytelling.
I. Anthony, Mitch. II. Title.
HG4621.W45 2000
332.6′068′8—dc21   99-049647

DEDICATION

To my father, Tom Anthony, salesman par excellence, who has taught me to believe in myself and to sell my own ideas.
—Mitch Anthony

To my father, Bob West, the most creative sales professional I've ever known, who has taught me to embrace risk as an enormous opportunity for creativity.
—Scott West

Contents

Preface

Why are some brokers and advisors thriving in an age while others are struggling to survive? Why do some seem to never get over the hump of building a bigger book of business? Why do some brokers struggle to keep up with all the referrals they get when others have to claw and dig just to get one referral?

We were determined to find the answers to those questions, to find exactly how top advisors sell. The characteristics we found in top advisors were both profound and simple:

1. The way they sold was illustrative and simple.
2. They excelled in relating and communicating with others.
3. They developed specialized audiences for their services.

The way top advisors sell is by simplifying matters, not complicating them. Many advisors purposefully add complexity to their presentation, thinking it raises their stature and indispensability in the eyes of their clients. This complicated approach, however, works against, not for, the advisor.

The top producers we found did just the opposite with amazing results. By using simple illustrations, anecdotes, and metaphors, they bring themselves and their ideas into the mental grasp of every client. Consequently, clients love talking to them and referring their friends as well.

We call this selling technique *storyselling*. We have come to believe that storyselling is the key to building a large and loyal book of business. It is a proven psychological fact that storytelling puts the mind in a light trancelike state and makes us more susceptible to influence. Everyone loves a good story. In this book we will teach you to tell the financial story.

In an age of online, do-it-yourself investing, people still yearn for mentoring, for guidance, and for affirmation. Many have gone the Lone Ranger route in investing because they haven't been able to find a broker who knows how to communicate effectively. Your success as an advisor hinges on your ability to communicate. Make the complex simple and understandable and you will never lack for clients. The storyselling truths and examples in this book will revolutionize the way you sell financial services and yourself.

Your success with clients doesn't hinge on being a better analyst but rather on being a better teacher, a better storyteller, and a master of the metaphor. Individuals will no longer tolerate being left in the dark, and they will gravitate to the advisors who excel in illuminating and communicating. In this book you will find the examples and techniques necessary to become an expert storyseller yourself.

Top advisors have a sincere concern and respect for people. Clients feel good after meeting with these advisors because they sense these advisors have their best interests at heart. The second section of this book reveals the relational magic top advisors exhibit: incisive questions, intuitive listening skills, the ability to read body language, a sense of humor, and down-to-earth humility. These pros recognize that what people really yearn for is respect.

We once heard a speaker say that all the people he had ever met had a sign hanging on their neck and that his own life had become a string of successes once he learned to read that sign. He said that when he was younger he was too caught up in himself to realize people were wearing this sign—much less to be able to read it. His life was far too important to be caught up in somebody else's world.

But a wiser man pointed out to him—as he did to us—that the sign around each person's neck actually says, "Help me feel important." He said, "No matter who they were, no matter how high they'd risen or how much they had, they all wear the same sign. Those who learn to recognize and respond to that sign will succeed."

We started looking for the sign on the people we knew and the people we met. We saw the sign on our wives and children. We saw it on clients and coworkers. We saw it on the paper boy. We saw it on the auto mechanic. We saw it in the eyes of our audiences.

This world has a way of wearing people down—it can be hard on them. It stereotypes them, categorizes them, and assigns numbers to them. But we want others to see us for the unique individuals we are.

The speaker was right—when you learn to read this sign, everything changes and success is inevitable.

You start with eye contact and attentiveness. You progress with a sincere and interested discovery process. It takes hold when your clients see that you have their best interests at heart. It is respect in the highest form. This book will show you how to demonstrate that sort of respect.

Finally, we found that top advisors have learned to focus and specialize their book of business into profitable such niches as the Affluent market, the Mature (65+) market, and the Woman's market. In Part 3 we have written about how these advisors are communicating with and prospering in those markets. By moving from a jack-of-all-trades, anybody-will-do advisor to a specialized expertise in profitable niches, these advisors have seen their book of business grow faster and larger than they ever imagined possible. In this book you will learn how to communicate with the growing markets of affluent, mature, and female investors, respectively.

Storyselling will help you become more expert at communicating, at relating, and at penetrating profitable markets—and make money in the process! Storyselling is about making an emotional connection with your clients' hopes and dreams by using illustrations and stories they can understand.

If, after reading this book, you'd like more illustrations, stories, and metaphors, or you have a favorite example you'd like to share, you can visit our Web site at www.storysellers.com.

ACKNOWLEDGMENTS

We want to acknowledge all the great people at VanKampen Consulting who have provided invaluable assistance in the preparation of Part 3 of this book. Thanks to Gary DeMoss, Brett VanBortel, Mark Lie, and Lisa Kueng for all their help, research, and encouragement. A special thanks to Lynn Guptill for her great organizational ability, willingness to help, and always cheerful demeanor.

Special thanks to Russ Alan Prince for his incisive research and insights into the Affluent market, to David Bach and Judith Tingley for their insights into the Woman's market.

A special thanks to all the authors and advisors who have contributed their storyselling insights, including John Sestina, Kay Shirley, Don Connelly, Allison Lewis, Roger Thomas, and many others too numerous to list here.

I (Mitch) would like to thank Debbie, my wife and editor of all my life's work, for her indefatigable encouragement and labor.

Special thanks to Dearborn editor Cindy Zigmund for her buoyant spirit, tactful tutoring, and belief in this project.

I'd like to thank Larry Foster of Universal Underwriters for affirming and encouraging my belief that metaphors and analogies are our most powerful selling tools.

I (Scott) would like to acknowledge broker Dick Stoker for his storyselling inspiration and for setting a remarkable example of how to make financial concepts come alive.

Finally, we would like to acknowledge those top storytelling professionals all over this country who have inspired us to articulate this powerful concept by their success every day in helping people fulfill their financial dreams.

PART ONE

How to Put Half of Your Client's Brain to Sleep

1 Why Statistics Don't Sell and Stories Do

A Short Course on Whole-Brain Persuasion

Some people use statistics like a drunken man uses a lamppost—for support rather than illumination.

ANONYMOUS

- If you rely on facts, statistics, and charts to sell, you're putting your clients to sleep.
- The presenter that appeals to both sides of the brain has twice the odds of winning the account.
- With the right stories and metaphors, you'll see better results.

What would happen if, starting today, you had to begin selling investment products (stocks, bonds, mutual funds, annuities, etc.) without the use of statistics, charts, rankings, or ratings? No Morningstar rankings, no Lipper or Mountain charts, no A.M. Best ratings, and no "finished 23d out of 179 similar funds" comments would be allowed in your presentation. Would you go mute? Would you suffer paralysis by analysis? Let's just pretend that this scenario did take place and ponder which alternative forms of presentation you would choose to use.

You might have to start telling stories, drawing pictures and illustrations, and using metaphors. You might start paying more attention to the individuality and personality of your clients and start focusing on discovering who they are and what's right for them. You might spend a lot less time talking and a lot more time listening. You might learn to intuitively read between the lines of what they are saying instead of force-feeding every client the same intellectual data.

Guess what? These are the things that the top producers in the financial services industry are doing right now. Highly successful brokers, planners, advisors, and investment bankers, the best of the best, have crafted the art of storyselling.

They came by it naturally. They intuitively solved the riddle of how to reach and teach clients what they need to know. Once that connection was made, they had found clients who trusted them for the long term. And they made a lot of money in the process.

SCIENCE AND ART

Warren Buffett once said that investing is part art and part science. We believe that selling investments is also part art and part science, but the majority of those selling investments put far too much emphasis on the science, which is not only boring clients to death but, because financial professionals are all using the same scientific charts and facts, have begun to sound like every other advisor and broker out there.

Financial services providers are familiar with the science of investments. However, we have found that an exclusively analytical scientific approach in explaining and selling investments has a half-brain appeal and, in fact, may be counterproductive. It may be counterproductive because when we get caught up in any form of analytical science, we begin to speak in jargon, which tends to confuse and intimidate most people. Many advisors are spewing jargon and investment cliches to uninitiated clients and don't realize the confusion and intimidation they are causing.

Highly successful storysellers have learned to simplify complex investment strategies and products. They have learned to relate these strategies and products to matters their clients can understand by using the phrase, "It's kind of like . . ." In this book we will share many of the stories, analogies, and metaphors that these successful financial professionals use to their own benefit and the benefit of their clients.

Warren Buffett is an excellent example of a natural storyseller. If you've read any interviews with, or books about, Buffett or read any of his letters to Berkshire-Hathaway shareholders, you have seen his instinct for, and lucid use of, metaphors, analogies, aphorisms, and anecdotes. His mind works this way and his shareholders appreciate it. He makes complex ideas understandable to people who are not versed in financial matters. This should be a primary communications goal of any financial advisor.

When asked a question before a congressional committee, Buffett began to relate a story toward the end of his testimony. The chairman who asked the question interrupted Buffett to say, "Not another story; can you just give us the answer?" Buffett replied, "I'm sorry, that's just the way my mind works." The truth is that when Buffett is explaining a matter, it is not only interesting, it is entertaining as well. He understands both the art and science of investing and explaining investments.

Buffett is such a shining example of storyselling that we have dedicated an entire chapter (Chapter 12) to his abilities and examples.

TURNING THE LIGHT ON

It is important for advisors to not only be knowledgeable but to be able to communicate as well. *All the knowledge and understanding in the world is useless if you can't effectively transfer and relate that understanding to your clients.* To become a more effective communicator, you must

- understand how the human brain works and how to capture and keep people's interest; and
- learn to integrate visual, imaginative, sensory, and emotive aspects in your client presentations through the art of storyselling.

As a result, you will gain tremendous confidence in your ability to communicate and connect with your clients. Your clients will feel a stronger bond to you as an advisor because you are not just an advisor who directs their assets but you are a teacher who simplifies and illuminates concepts they once found confusing. Their personal confidence level is now raised because of their increased understanding, and their confidence and trust in you is raised because of this connection you have established. You have turned on the light about a topic that has confounded and perplexed them in the past.

> "If there are 500,000 investment professionals in America, I'm sure 494,000 of them sound the same."
> —Client comment

"If there are 500,000 investment professionals in America, I'm sure 494,000 of them sound the same."—Client comment
  I was riding in an airport limo next to a man who told me he was an executive in a growing software company. He asked me what I did.

When he learned I was involved in the financial services industry, he launched into a diatribe about the confusion of knowing where to invest in a crowded, confusing, and redundant marketplace. "All these companies sound the same. The same charts, the same statistics, the same pitches. I can't tell one from the other. And figuring out what's right for me, well, how are you gonna know what's right for you, really?"

I replied, "Let me ask you a question that's a little off the topic. Let's say you had an opportunity to buy an exclusive condo on the lakefront and there were only two units left. One is on the top floor where you have this inspiring panoramic view, and the other one is on the bottom floor where you can get out quickly in case of a fire. Which one do you think you'd buy?"

I watched him scratch his head. I could see from his eyes that the wheels were turning. He grinned and said, "I want the view. I'll take the risk. For me, it's about the view."

"I bring it up," I offered, "because you sounded confused about what type of fund was right for you. With your answer I think I could point you to the type of fund that matches your risk tolerance."

"I like it," he said. "Nobody's approached me like that but when you put it that way, it's easy to decide."

I was amazed at how his demeanor changed with this metaphor. He was intrigued. The perplexed look left his face. I could see his imagination running with the metaphor. Before we parted company he said, "I'd be inclined to listen to someone who explained things that way." Here was an intelligent executive who wanted financial matters made as simple as possible.

This is just one of the many examples of storyselling, the use of metaphors to increase illumination, stir the imagination, and promote a decision that fits each client's comfort zone. Why does this approach work? Because it appeals to *both* sides of the brain. It gets us fully involved in the decision, intellectually, imaginatively, emotionally, and intuitively.

Before we go any further, we must explain what it is about the human brain that makes this approach so effective. We will also use a storyselling approach (metaphor) to make the lesson more memorable.

THE METAPHORIC MAP OF YOUR BRAIN

Think of the map of your brain like a map of the United States (Figure 1.1)—not as you would look at the map but as if you were looking out from the map. On your left side is Washington, D.C., with its rules, regulations, and bureaucracies with a need to control. Then, there is Wall Street analysis with its number-crunching accountants and economists. Some basic functions of the left side of your brain are logic, reasoning, counting, planning, organizing, inspecting, and analyzing.

On the right side of this map is Hollywood with its imagination, visual stimulation, and emotion-packed stories about relationships and experiences. Hollywood stirs us, entertains us (Washington, D.C., entertains us but does so unwittingly), and moves us in dramatic fashion. Some basic functions of the right side of your brain are imagining, seeing the big picture, relating, laughing, remembering, and feeling.

Just as Washington, D.C., and Hollywood are many miles apart geographically and in function, so too are the left and right sides of your brain apart. Even though they are geographically joined, they are many miles apart in function. The way we

FIGURE 1.1   The Metaphoric Map of Your Brain

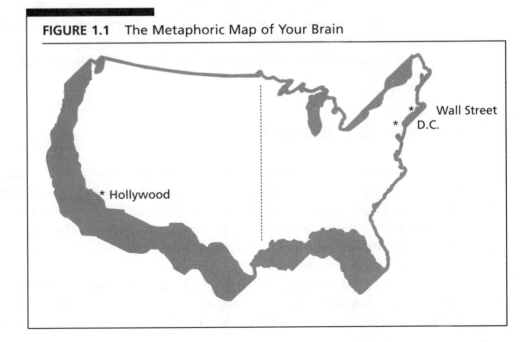

communicate to those two sides of the brain is no less than the difference between science and art.

The two sides of our brain are joined by 300 to 400 million fiber-optic connectors. At any given time, those connectors are transmitting millions of pieces of information from the two sides of our brain with their two distinct ways of viewing our world. A computer has not been built that can mimic the instantaneous and diverse processing that takes place in our brain spontaneously. In a conversation with a client our brain is receiving and sorting input from the client's words and body language while simultaneously preparing and organizing the information and ideas we wish to communicate. We take this complex process for granted but it is an amazing process. The truth is that we have not come close to utilizing the capabilities we possess in our thinking or communicating skills.

Perhaps you've heard of the psychology professor who told his class that scientists had discovered that we use only 10 percent of our brain's potential. A student asked, "Excuse me, sir, but isn't there a 90 percent chance that they're wrong about that?"

Our concern is the possibility that we might be off the mark 90 percent of the time in the way we communicate financial concepts and solutions to our clients. We know we are usually off by 50 percent because presentation materials and dialogue are predominately tailored to the left side of the brain—the number-crunching center. We believe this book will help you to expand your brain's potential to think and therefore communicate in clearer, more understandable ways to your clients.

CLIENTS IN THE DARK

The more knowledgeable you become about how human brains work, the simpler but more effective your presentations will become. This is just the opposite of what many people would expect. Usually, the more people know about a given topic, the more complex and detailed their explanations become, which is why we often fail to truly connect with the audience in our presentations. We have presented over their heads—and that causes mistrust.

In exit interviews with clients and potential clients we asked, "Did you walk away with a clear understanding of what your financial advisor was talking about?" We often heard, "No, some things confused me." When we asked their advisors how the consultation went, they would often remark, "I think it went pretty well." The only opinion that matters here is the client's.

What mistakes do we make that cause clients to walk away confused and in the dark? Some advisors purposely use complex language, thinking they elevate themselves in the eyes of the client. "Isn't he or she intelligent?" is the thought they are hoping for, but what this approach often produces is intimidation and confusion. As a retired executive told me after visiting a "real smart" advisor, "He intimidated me with all his industry jargon and complex strategies. I took my business elsewhere because I don't feel comfortable entrusting my fate to people who intimidate me."

Other advisors unwittingly confuse and intimidate clients by

- using too much trade jargon; or
- assuming clients know or understand more than they actually do (clients will often act as though they understand matters when they actually don't). I have heard many clients express their confusion after a meeting with an advisor. "What did she mean by that?" "How does that work?" "I didn't quite get what he was trying to say there." They didn't say a word in the session because of the natural fear of appearing stupid or foolish.

We will deal more fully with the issue of jargon in Chapter 5. For now, suffice it to say that too many advisors are using jargon as a presentation crutch because they have not learned more effective means of communicating.

When we bring up the issue of simplifying presentations, there might even be some who buck up and say, "I'm a professional. I don't want to appear simplistic or average. Clients come to me because I know more than they do." When we encounter this type of mind-set, we're reminded of the Australian who said, "You'd be six foot tall if you weren't five foot up yourself!"

Of course you are a professional. So are doctors and lawyers, but we still prefer the ones who can come down off of their eight-syllable soapbox and speak to us in a way that illuminates rather than confounds.

When pondering the pure intelligence of simplicity, ponder some of history's greatest minds. Jesus explained complex spiritual matters with simple parables like "The Lost Coin" and "The Mustard Seed." Ben Franklin dealt with the complex issues of independence with stories from Poor Richard in his yearly almanac. Einstein knew how to explain complex scientific principles in ways everyone could relate to. Consider this gem from Einstein on the theory of relativity: "When you place your hand on a hot stove for a second, it feels like an hour. When you sit on a bench with a pretty girl for an hour it feels like a second—that's relativity!" It was also Einstein who said, "Things should be made as simple as possible but not any simpler."

The world's greatest minds have known that metaphors, anecdotes, humor, and illustrations are the more potent tools of teaching and persuasion. We will follow their lead.

We are confronting this idea of simplicity in presentation early on because, at its roots, this is *what storyselling is all about—making complex ideas understandable.* Once these ideas are understood, the next step is establishing relevance into the life of the client. The KISS rule—keep it simple, stupid—is a foundational rule practiced by top producers in every sales realm. If you break that rule, you do so at your own risk.

Readin', Writin', and 'Rithmetic

One major reason we are not better communicators is because of the way we have been trained to think. Had we been taught to think *with* all our brain, we would also have learned to communicate *to* the whole brain as well. As you will see in subsequent charts, our educational and business cultures place a heavy emphasis on left-brain functions to the neglect of the right-brain functions that are critical to our success. Communication, of which selling is one form, is just one area where this imbalance has cost us dearly.

As you can see in Figure 1.2, our education has been heavily weighted toward left-brain functions. The farther down the educational road we go, the more left-leaning the focus. By the time one exits graduate school, thinking processes have become something like the leaning tower of Pisa! From first grade on, the emphasis is on the 3 Rs—pronouncing syllables, writing the alphabet, and counting numbers. Our educational system aims to produce graduates who can crunch numbers, analyze facts, argue logically, find problems, and implement logical solutions.

Most businesses perpetuate the left-brain obsession by emphasizing the bottom line and by aiming to reach that bottom line through organizing, managing, inspecting, and controlling. These left-brain processes are necessary in any successful business, but the irony here is that these same companies tell their people that what they need to increase their bottom line are creativity, innovation, vision for the future, customer insight, persuasive selling, and sensitive service. These profit-building attributes are exclusive functions of the right brain and are hindered, if not totally crippled, by narrow left-brain thinking and many management practices.

FIGURE 1.2   Brain Functions

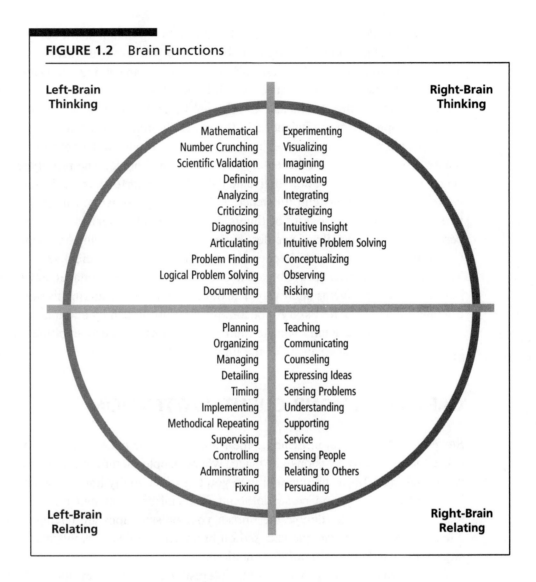

Left-Brain Thinking	Right-Brain Thinking
Mathematical	Experimenting
Number Crunching	Visualizing
Scientific Validation	Imagining
Defining	Innovating
Analyzing	Integrating
Criticizing	Strategizing
Diagnosing	Intuitive Insight
Articulating	Intuitive Problem Solving
Problem Finding	Conceptualizing
Logical Problem Solving	Observing
Documenting	Risking

Left-Brain Relating	Right-Brain Relating
Planning	Teaching
Organizing	Communicating
Managing	Counseling
Detailing	Expressing Ideas
Timing	Sensing Problems
Implementing	Understanding
Methodical Repeating	Supporting
Supervising	Service
Controlling	Sensing People
Adminstrating	Relating to Others
Fixing	Persuading

THE ROOTS OF SALES SUCCESS

In selling, there is no denying that analysis, number crunching, logic, and organization play a necessary role. However, these left-brain functions constitute, at best, about 10 to 20 percent of the critical mass necessary for sales success. The other 80 to 90 percent comes from right-brain functions, which play primary roles in the sales realm. In sales, we talk about the need for people skills because we are selling ourselves. People skills are a right-brain function. We talk about being able to read people. This reading is a right-brain function. We talk about sensing, skilled listening, communication flair and skill, intuitive problem solving, innovation, and humor when describing highly successful salespeople—and the very best do possess these traits. All of these traits and abilities are based in the right side of the brain.

Most people are fairly balanced in their right-brain and left-brain orientation. Many people who naturally excel in sales, however, lean toward a right-brain dominance from whence these necessary sales skills are rooted. The prototype sales achiever is an imaginative and motivated risk taker, a colorful communicator, an incisive questioner, an insightful listener, and a likable personality. Chances are this person also likes to have a lot of things going on (multitasker), is passionate and persuasive, abhors detail and needless paperwork, can't stand being on a short leash (micromanaged), and needs freedom to improvise and try out creative strategies. These individuals detest being boxed in and love to respond spontaneously to situations and solve problems intuitively. The more an individual leans to this right-brain orientation, the more necessary it becomes to be surrounded by administrative assistance to attend to detail, manage multiple activities, organize ambitious schedules, and generally keep aware of the linear world in which the individual lives.

CAPTURING YOUR CLIENTS' ATTENTION

Storyselling focuses on influencing the right side of the client's brain. Why? Because that is where decisions get made, where people picture and buy into what we are selling. This technique will help you to exponentially improve your ability to articulate, clarify, and persuade about financial concepts and products. This technique will literally double the impact your presentations are having on your clients because the technique is based on brain science that demonstrates how to engage the whole brain in our presentations.

How do you mesmerize your clients' interest? How is trust developed? The answers to these questions are evident once you see the discoveries of modern brain science and how these discoveries relate to selling.

Ned Herrmann in his book *The Whole-Brain Business Book* offers a chart (see Figure 1.3) called "Our Four Different Selves" that shows the different shades of personality we display from the two sides of our brain:

- Our rational self
- Our safekeeping self

FIGURE 1.3 Our Four Different Selves

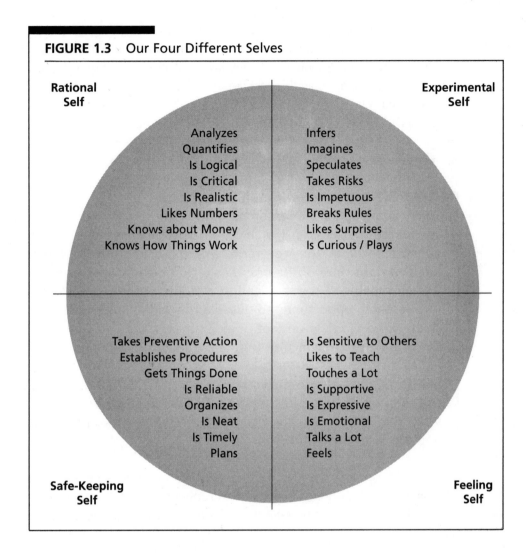

Rational Self	Experimental Self
Analyzes	Infers
Quantifies	Imagines
Is Logical	Speculates
Is Critical	Takes Risks
Is Realistic	Is Impetuous
Likes Numbers	Breaks Rules
Knows about Money	Likes Surprises
Knows How Things Work	Is Curious / Plays

Safe-Keeping Self	Feeling Self
Takes Preventive Action	Is Sensitive to Others
Establishes Procedures	Likes to Teach
Gets Things Done	Touches a Lot
Is Reliable	Is Supportive
Organizes	Is Expressive
Is Neat	Is Emotional
Is Timely	Talks a Lot
Plans	Feels

- Our experimental self
- Our feeling self

As is customary in our culture, we pay an inordinate amount of attention to the left-brain issues of rationale and safekeeping and often neglect the experimental and feeling side of ourselves. We direct clients to volumes of numbers, statistics, and small print. Many of these clients give the materials a cursory glance or ignore it. They want you to illuminate them and relate to them on a personal basis. They want you to discover the individuals that they are. They want you to tailor a program that is specific to their unique circumstances. Their circumstances may not seem unique to you, but clients feel that they are in specifically unique circumstances.

Note that speculation and risk taking are actions that come from the right-brain experimental self. What is investing if it is not about speculating and taking risks? To properly communicate to those right-brain functions, we need to speak a language the right side of the brain can relate to. Statistics, numbers, and prospectuses are not that language! Yes, they play a role—a supporting role, not a leading one.

Thirty years ago brain researcher Roger Sperry, with his associates, conducted split-brain research on patients who had been having epileptic seizures. They severed the corpus callosum that connects the left and right sides of the brain. As a result, the two sides of the brain were incapable of communicating with each other and provided a rare research opportunity to observe the various functions of the two sides of the brain. In one set of experiments, they hooked each side of the brain up to an electroencephalogram (EEG) and studied the left and right brain responses to various stimuli. When they read statistics and facts, the left side stirred with electrical activity but the right side of the brain literally went to sleep or was idle. Researchers then told a story and immediately the right side of the brain was fully engaged and the left side continued its interest.

What's our point? The materials and presentation style many financial professionals use is a half-brained approach to selling because it only engages 50 percent of the potential attention the client has to give. Half the client's brain remains asleep.

RISKS AND DECISIONS

We want clients to measure risk, to look into the future and visualize how today's decision will affect them 20 years from now. These are abilities that they possess in the right side of their head and we simply need to learn the language that will trigger those abilities.

Typically, when we sell financial products we speak the language of the rational left brain, which is fine to a point, but the left side of the brain does not decide on anything! It will analyze from here to eternity. The more information you give the left brain to analyze, the more it will procrastinate. Left-brain dominant people are those who can't get enough information and have a terrible time making decisions.

People analyze with their left side. They agonize over information and numbers, but they don't decide. The right side puts it all together and forms a picture, gets a feeling, and then makes the leap. Once the decision has been made, the left side kicks in and wants to get it done with planning and organizing.

Once you understand this point—that decision making and risk taking are a right-brain function—you will immediately see the relevance of learning to speak the language of the right brain. Your livelihood depends on your ability to do so. Our next chapter will show you *how* to speak this right-brain language of persuasion.

2 | Learning to Speak the Language of the Right Brain

The classic mistake we make in persuasion is trying to evoke right-brain responses (action, risk, decision) by using left-brain stimuli (numbers, facts, history). This is equal to asking individuals to look into their future by using a microscope—they can't see past their noses. To look into the future, to make a decision, or to take a risk requires a telescope. Storyselling uses the telescopic mental tools that help clients see and feel—before they act.

Figure 2.1 illustrates left-brain and right-brain views of the world. Here you'll find the clues necessary to effectively speak the language of the right brain.

STORYSELLING TRIGGERS

This chart reveals the triggers that release the "paralysis by analysis" stress clients feel when they are trying to make a decision. In selling situations, the right brain needs and desires the following:

- Context (personal relevance)
- The big picture (long-term relevance)
- Humor
- Images
- Visual stimulation
- Emotional affirmation
- Affirmation of values
- Metaphors
- Stories
- A comfortable feeling about you

FIGURE 2.1 Left-Brain–Right-Brain View of the World

Left Brain	Right Brain
Breaks into pieces	Forms into whole
Backward looking	Forward looking
Looks at text	Looks at context
Seeks detail	Seeks big picture
Takes everything literally	Understands humor
Literal, proven examples	Metaphorical examples
Triggered with information	Triggered with images
Businesslike (judging/critical)	Relational
Rational	Intuitive
Gathers information	Understands meaning and relevance
Stirred by facts, statistics, and claims	Stirred by emotions, beliefs, and hopes
Analyzes	Decides
Stimulated by data	Stimulated by stories
Seeks detail	Seeks big picture
Focused on words	Focused on tone of voice and body language
Auditory	Visual
Finds problems	Searches for solutions

Context

Think of establishing context in this way: "We are going to read the last page of the book before we try to write a table of contents. We're going to start with an end in mind. Now, tell me everything you want to accomplish . . . that is how we want this story to turn out."

Like the archaeologist who discovers a shard and immediately begins to visualize the entire ancient pot, so the brain searches for the personal significance of the ideas or suggestions it hears.

If context is not clearly established up front, the client will start questioning (internally) the relevance of the various products and ideas you are talking about. This sounds like an elementary point, but we can't count the number of presentations we have witnessed where the context was not established up front and the client had to stop and ask halfway through the presentation, "Now, how does this tie in?" *Establish the context at the beginning clearly and continue to refer back to it at key points in your presentation.* The right side of the brain wants to know how each piece of text fits into the context. If it does not recognize the context, the right side of the brain ignores the information.

The Big Picture

This is an area—presenting the big picture—where many advisors already do well. They do it by talking about the entire portfolio and the need for diversification. They also do it by displaying charts and graphs that show the performance of funds over 10 years or the performance of equities over the last 60 years. The right side of the brain wants to know how the particular strategy or product fits into the larger scheme of the overall strategy or timeline.

Humor

Ponder this physiological fact: laughter and stress cannot occupy the same space at the same time. Financial decisions are stressful to make. Even after a decision is made, the mind begins to second guess with a litany of "what ifs." Laughter diffuses stress. Humor puts matters into their proper perspective. By using humor, we don't mean telling canned jokes or presenting puns. Humor is better introduced into the atmosphere by our attitude, manner, and approach. Start by smiling. Check your own tension in the mirror before your client walks in the room. Laugh easily. Don't hurry. Share a good story that has humorous aspects. If you're married and/or have children, such stories are bountiful and people can relate to them.

After 20 years of presentations to groups ranging from one person to five thousand, I am more convinced of the power of humor in persuasion than of any other form of communication. Humor opens the door to emotional buy-in. Laughter puts the audience at ease and creates a bond with the presenter. It puts them on the same page. Thoughts of "I can relate to that," "He's one of us," "I've had that kind of thought myself" is what the twinkle in the eye of the person laughing is saying. Discomfort is dissipated. Stress is released. After people laugh, their attention level becomes heightened and magnetic. They don't want to miss the next punch line. People love being entertained in situations where they don't expect it.

We think this topic is important enough that we have dedicated Chapter 6, "How Self-Deprecation and Wit Will Get You Further Than Self-Promotion," to this aspect of presenting.

Images: Pictures, Drawings, Cartoons

If a good picture is worth a thousand words, then a few good pictures could save you a lot of time and talk. Later in this book we will display some images and relate them to investment themes. You may wish to use these images in client presentations to clarify issues or to differentiate strategies. However, when we speak of images, we don't refer exclusively to printed images but to images in the mind as well. Pictures formed by the imagination of your clients are exceedingly more powerful than any picture you could show them. You help to paint these pictures in their imagination with provocative questions about their life and experience, with entertaining and interesting stories, and by the application of relevant metaphors. The provocative question is a topic we cover in depth in Chapter 5, "How Socrates Can Help You Reach Your Sales Quota."

Visual Stimulation

The pencil may be your most powerful selling tool! If you know how to use it, that is. A presenter who knows how to integrate the drawing of images and outlining of ideas into his or her client presentation is like a teacher before a captive class. We have studied the dynamic shift in attention level and body language when the pencil on paper technique is used. If the audience had been leaning backward, they are now leaning forward. If their eyes were starting to drift or gloss over, they are now drawn to the pencil's movements and the logic and lessons it brings. We have watched advisors draw pyramids, houses, cars, chairs, trees, and a plethora of other analogies for the plan they are developing and the philosophy on which it is based. The analogy doesn't matter as long as you can make it relevant. The audience participates like students. They will point to the analogy on the board at different junctures and refer back to it. By using this method, the presenter is able to establish a "language" with which their clients' right brain can connect.

> The pencil may be your most powerful selling tool! If you know how to use it, that is. A presenter who knows how to integrate the drawing of images and outlining of ideas into his or her client presentation is like a teacher before a captive class.

Emotional Affirmation

No question is as important as, How do you feel about this? That question is more incisive than, What do you think about this? Why? Because emotion precedes logic when we hear others' ideas. The choices we make are based on about 80 percent emotion and 20 percent logic or rationale.

If every advisor were properly trained to read the body language of their clients (eyes, facial movement, posture), they would realize that many of the ideas they present, companies they mention, or stocks they recommend trigger a veiled, emo-

Over and over we have seen brokers and advisors make purchase suggestions and be so absorbed in their presentation that they miss the body language signs of stop, yield, and even U-turn. If you miss these signs, your presentation will fail. If you're lucky, your client will tell you about your navigational error—but probably not.

tional reaction. Usually clients won't state this reaction aloud unless asked about it. If advisors don't know how to pick up on these tacit messages, they will venture onto thin ice or even step on land mines, thus sabotaging their hopes for success. The next chapter, "What's Your Gut Feeling? How Decisions Really Get Made," will discuss in greater depth the topic of body language. Suffice it to say that far too many advisors place too little emphasis on feelings and too much on logic. Yet we have seen time and time again that buying is more of an emotional decision than a logical one.

Research has revealed that when people are questioned about their experiences, the associated emotion in the brain is triggered first, followed by the associated facts. Emotion always precedes fact in the human brain's response. People feel first and rationalize later.

Over and over we have seen brokers and advisors make purchase suggestions and be so absorbed in their presentation that they miss the body language signs of stop, yield, and even U-turn. If you miss these signs, your presentation will fail. If you're lucky, your client will tell you about your navigational error—but probably not.

People have either positive, neutral, or negative feelings about any company or product you present. You're wise to discover what those feelings are.

We once watched a broker recommend the stock of a well-known and highly successful retail store to a retired couple. As soon as he mentioned the company, we saw an eyebrow go up. The broker went on to describe this company's record, marketing savvy, and future prospects. When he was through, the couple said nothing and nodded slightly as if to gesture that they agreed—but with skeptical eyes.

We later asked, "Have you had any experience with this company?"

"Oh, yes!" was their reply and they spent five minutes telling us about two negative experiences they had in this retail store. They didn't care how good the company's story was—their personal experience emotionally superseded it.

We warn of negative emotions, but clients come for positive emotional affirmation. They often have suspicions about what they might or could do but need someone to second the motion. Even well-studied, do-it-yourself investors will come to advisors for affirmation. One advisor mentioned that one of these do-it-yourselfers came to him to ask how much he would charge for an hour of his time once a year to get feedback on his investment strategies. The investor knew as much as the advisor on many topics, but what he needed was to lie on the couch of a financial psychiatrist. Everyone looks for emotional affirmation and are willing to pay for it, figuring it's a small price to pay for curing insomnia.

Emotions play a much greater role than logic in the average person's investment decisions. Your ability to sense is just as important as your ability to rationalize. Empathy will, in the long run, pay you richer dividends than will intelligence.

Affirmation of Values

All people have a very idiosyncratic set of beliefs, principles, or values that they try to follow when making investment decisions. It's advantageous to discover what those principles or values are before you begin promoting an idea or strategy that may or may not match a client's particular set of values. Principles and values have deep-seated emotions attached to them. There are significant reasons clients hold to these principles. If you can discover and connect with your clients' values, you will have forged a philosophical connection that will not be easily broken. People often choose or refuse to purchase on the basis of a values match or mismatch with the advisor or salesperson.

I always thought I wanted a luxury car or a big luxury truck, and, once in awhile, I would go out and look at them. I liked what I saw, I liked what I felt. The money wasn't a problem. But something inside of me wouldn't let me do it. It was a feeling I had. I sorted it out and realized what it was. It was a matter of principle for me. I could not bring myself to pay more for a vehicle than I had paid for my first house. That might sound silly to a lot of people, but for me it was a value I couldn't violate

ANDREW T., CLIENT

All people have an idiosyncratic set of values and principles they choose to live by. No two are exactly alike. We have heard countless stories from clients who were upset and offended by offers to purchase company stocks, specific funds, or products that infringed on an emotionally charged value or principle. These offers were made by unwitting brokers and advisors who had no idea how passionate a refusal they would arouse. Worse yet is the scenario in which the potential client voices no objection or refusal but simply walks away. Here are some examples:

- The WWII vet who was offered an international fund specializing in a nation that had sunk his ship in the Pacific
- The woman who was offered shares in an automobile company whose manufacturing error had resulted in an accident that caused her husband back pain for much of his life
- The couple who was offered a mutual fund by a company whose agent had offended them years before leaving a bad taste in their mouths
- The woman who was offended by being offered an investment opportunity in a company that had received poor marks on its environmental record

For these people, not only were these issues emotionally charged but they were matters of principles as well. They did not choose to garner growth or gain from these particular concerns—no matter how they might prosper from doing so.

In Chapter 5, "How Socrates Can Help You Reach Your Sales Quota," we will reveal the question that you can ask to make sure that your strategies and product offerings create a *values match*. A growing number of people see their money and what they do with it as an extension of who they are. They have established a spiritual and philosophical link between their souls and their money.

This money/soul connection is the reason why socially responsible investing (SRI) has become such a prodigious investment category. According to an article in the *Dow Jones Investment Advisor* (March 1999), socially responsible investing is now a very big business. One source, *Green Money Journal,* puts total SRI investments at $1.2 trillion—almost 10 percent of all money invested yearly in America. According to the Social Investing Forum, which runs the numbers every two years, total assets devoted to SRI in 1997 doubled from the 1995 total.

For example, many people have decided that they don't want to invest in tobacco companies. Having learned this, many mutual funds made it known that they wouldn't invest in tobacco. Some companies, such as Pioneer, had been adhering to this philosophy since 1929, but it didn't show up in their prospectuses or marketing materials. You can be sure that it does appear today.

Lutheran Brotherhood, whose funds are available only to certified Lutherans, has done quite well with in-flows and returns with its "no sin" approach that excludes tobacco, alcohol, and gambling concerns.

Have you been asked by a client to screen against various causes or principles? Do you attempt to make such clarifications? This is just one more piece of proof that investors are making their investment decisions from the right side of their brain.

Metaphors

Metaphors are "word pictures" that give language power and richness by involving our senses in the experience.

GABRIELLE LUSSER RICA

If you have an accurate and deep knowledge of your subject matter, you can multiply many times over the impact of your communication by moving from the literal to the analogic. Through the proper metaphor you can reveal the depth of your knowledge and the wisdom of your strategy. Mastering the metaphoric takes you from the realm of just another rep to financial guru. *People attach sagacity and significance to those who are able to distill complex ideas into word pictures.*

Warren Buffett was once asked about investing in a bull market. His answer: "A rising tide lifts all boats. It's not until the tide goes out that you realize who's swimming naked."

We have studied clients' responses to this metaphor. A grin breaks out on their faces. Their eyes shift. They are picturing it! The image strikes their funny bone. They will nod and affirm the wisdom of the metaphor. The right side of their brain is fully activated. You've got their attention. They learned something in an entertaining, illustrative manner. You could have made a literal statement like, "You have to be careful and selective when investing in a bull market," but without the picture, how much impact would that statement have had?

However, you can make that literal statement after the use of the metaphor and you've made a connection in both sides of their brain. You gave them a picture they will not forget and a rule along with it. You then continue your metaphoric presentation with, "Mr. and Mrs. Jones, the thing I want to find for you are companies that won't be swimming naked if and when the tide goes out. We know that it is the nature of things for the tide to surge and ebb, and we want to be in a good position, no matter which way the water is flowing."

Clients sense wisdom here. This is not hype, blind optimism, or wishful thinking they are hearing but wisdom and experience. Why do they feel this? Because you took a topic they do not understand (equities, values, market fluctuations) and related it to something that they do understand (the tide).

The secret of great teachers in every realm: they bring understanding and clarity through application of the appropriate metaphor. In Chapter 7, "Making the Intuitive Leap with Your Client," we will demonstrate how advisors have used this technique with great success. They have found that the pocketbook opens up no

The secret of great teachers in every realm: they bring understanding and clarity through application of the appropriate metaphor.

wider than the mind's breadth of understanding. When you bring illumination to the table, your clients answer with trust.

This point is the philosophical epicenter of our book. Illuminate your clients like no advisor before you and they will have no need for an advisor after you. This illumination process cannot and will not happen through the display of numbers and voluminous prospectuses. This illumination happens when you make multiple connections in the right side of your clients' brains. There's a fairly good chance that they have not had such an enlightening experience with a financial professional before you.

A metaphor is a translation from one mental language to another, from the literal to the analogic. Its power is the instant understanding it brings by reason of the translation . . . with understanding there will be a direct hit.

NED HERRMANN

This book is designed to give you an arsenal of metaphors to use in reaching the diversity of clients (the affluent, women, matures, boomers, etc.) and in addressing the diversity of investment issues and products. Your clients don't want a statistician, an analyst, or an investment schill. They want an advisor, a counselor, a teacher, a coach.

The advisor of the future may be equal parts Peter Lynch and personal coach.

OLIVIA MELLON, *INVESTMENT ADVISOR MAGAZINE*

Mastering the art of integrating metaphorical speech into your presentations will increase your stature in the eyes of your clients and deepen the trust and respect in their hearts. This principle holds especially true with the 65+ market that we explore in depth in Chapter 10, "Telling the Story of the 65+."

Stories

People love a good story and they love to hear it told well. Ronald Reagan endeared himself to the nation with his storytelling ability. Paul Harvey possesses unheard of longevity in radio because of his storytelling prowess. In fact, when Paul Harvey gives his version of the news, you can hardly tell where the news ends and the product ads begin. His delivery is so seamless that by the time you figure it out, he's already captured your interest. We would all do well to study his techniques.

When you say, "Let me tell you a story . . . ," the right side of the brain, as well as the left side, is at full alert. You have the complete resources of the brain focused on what is to come next. We often hear advisors saying they want to double their business. These advisors can start by doubling their impact in every client presentation. Storyselling doubles the impact of your presentation in a client's brain. Stories are a powerful medium but, unfortunately, storytelling is somewhat of a lost art. The essence of the storyselling approach is integrating the use of metaphors and anecdotes to deliver your message.

We have found that the most successful advisors practice this approach intuitively. They have discovered which stories pack the most punch. They have discovered that lessons and morals in stories, being implicitly rather than explicitly stated, are more readily received.

We love to hear stories about how others have succeeded, but sometimes we want to hear how they have failed. While we listen to a story, we first try to imagine what we are hearing, and we then try to find an emotional connection with the aspects of the story that we relate to. John Grisham's novels sell and movie theaters continue to fill because of people's love affair with a good story.

We all have stories to tell. Where did we come from? How did we get to where we are? Why did we decide to do what we do? There are many significant stories we all have to tell in response to those questions. The answers a client offers will reveal much about your client that we may want or need to know. Later we discuss how to cajole clients into telling their significant stories. By asking questions that very few advisors ask, you will hear stories that very few people get to hear. Hearing these stories is a big step toward establishing an unbreakable bond with your clients. Their life, their history, their values, their hopes and dreams, their emotional triggers are revealed in these stories.

If you can tell stories that embody your philosophy, wisdom, and commitment, and can evoke stories that reveal the same aspects of your clients, you are a born storyseller. If you'd like to get better, then stay along for the read.

A COMFORTABLE FEELING ABOUT YOU

Trust—this is at the heart of the client-advisor relationship. With the 65+ market, having a trusted advisor is ranked as high as receiving solid returns on money. People seek to do business with individuals they have a good feeling about. The right side of the brain, where risk and decision are launched, is not looking at your credentials; it is observing your body language. It is not caught up in your impressive recitation of facts and figures; it is reading between the lines. The right side of the brain is putting together what it observes in your eyes, your mannerisms, your tone and demeanor and is going to render an intuitive verdict that clients will follow even without a logical reason. "I just have a feeling," people will tell you—and they usually follow that feeling or are haunted by ignoring its ominous voice.

> **Clients will buy** inferior products from people they trust more often than they will buy superior products from people they don't trust. The ultimate consumer goal is to buy the best product from the best representative.

Clients will buy inferior products from people they trust more often than they will buy superior products from people they don't trust. The ultimate consumer goal is to buy the best product from the best representative.

In the next chapter we detail how to ensure that people get the right feeling about you. This objective can only be reached by first learning to listen to the people smarts coming from the right side of your brain. You must learn to read and trust the intuitive sirens and caution lights you pick up in your client presentations. You must pay very careful attention to the impression you are giving others. You must possess the humility to ask others how you are doing and how you can improve.

THE REPORT CARD

I know of one advisor who grades himself after every client presentation. The grade is based strictly on how he felt he did in his communication with his clients. A day or two later, he calls his clients to see how they felt about the meeting. Did they have the understanding they needed? Did they feel assured with the choices that were made? This advisor understands that the clients' being comfortable with him as a person hinges on his ability to communicate. This comfort level between client and advisor should supersede all other issues in the mind of the advisor if he or she hopes to have long-term relationships.

Can you make better connections with your clients by connecting with their imagination, emotions, hopes, and dreams? Absolutely. The buttons you need to push to connect with their imagination, emotions, hopes, and dreams are in the right side of their brain and are connected through those methods we have described here. Storyselling is an approach that will keep your clients from ever becoming bored and will leave an indelible and positive mark in their memory about your competence as an advisor.

3 | What's Your Gut Feeling? How Decisions Really Get Made

When I see confusion or hesitation in the eyes of, or consternation on the face of, a client making an investment decision, I like to stop and ask, "What's your gut feeling about this?" The client will begin expressing certain fears, uncertainties, and doubts. Often the client will turn the question on me and ask, "What's your gut feeling on this?" If our gut feelings can agree, he or she walks out a satisfied client.

BILL Y., BROKER

CLIENT PRIORITIES

In a recent study by Investor's Research, Inc., clients were asked what their priorities were with their financial advisor. Here were their top six priorities:

1. Understand my situation
2. Educate me
3. Respect my assets (no matter how small)
4. Solve my problem—don't sell me product
5. Monitor my progress
6. Keep in touch

Take note that all six of these priorities are relational in nature. People desire a stronger relational bond with the individual who is helping to determine their financial destiny. Making a favorable impression as a human being supersedes making a favorable impression as an advisor in the eyes of the client. Your personality and method of relating is going to have a pivotal emotional impact—one way or another.

GUT FEELING

It doesn't seem to matter what sort of decision we are making—a purchase, a career, a move, or a negotiation—we all instinctively rely on this gut feeling for guidance. Logic and rationale, although held in the highest esteem in our society, are not the trusted linchpins of our most important decisions. In fact, we almost always seem to make decisions based on our gut feelings and then align the necessary logic behind that feeling. The intuitive gut feeling is the engine of the decision train, and logic and rationale are the cars it pulls behind.

Yet in many of our presentations to clients we spend too much time filling the rationale boxcars with facts and figures and not enough time trying to influence the engine that pulls the train—the gut feeling. A powerful presentation first influences the emotion that drives the decision and then adds logic as the client asks for it.

Storyselling recognizes this simple fact: *Buying decisions hinge more on feeling than they do on fact.* Does this mean we ignore facts? Absolutely not! The facts simply become a part of our story—but not *the* story. Facts and numbers alone make for a dull story simply because they appeal largely to the side of our brain that acts like a computer. We want to appeal to this side to a degree, but to get to a decision we need to appeal to the side of the brain that acts like a movie screen. We want to ignite belief, trust, assurance, hope, and even passion for the ideas or products we are describing. The storyselling approach attempts to breathe life into facts and statistics as they play a supporting role in the story of the product you are selling. It is important to first focus on getting the right feelings across. Right feelings lead to positive perceptions, and positive perceptions are the reason people buy any product or service. You must focus on influencing how clients *feel* to become a successful presenter.

> **F**acts and numbers alone make for a dull story simply because they appeal largely to the side of our brain that acts like a computer. We want to appeal to this side to a degree, but to get to a decision we need to appeal to the side of the brain that acts like a movie screen.

In the following example we asked two brokers to sell a mutual fund that was weighted in technology, health care, and financial services equities. The second presentation was given by a broker who had received training in storyselling.

Broker #1:

Mr. and Mrs. Jones, one thing I look for in a mutual fund is a manager who is investing in areas I believe will show some growth and at least a five-year record of solid returns.

Now this fund *(he pulls out a prospectus)* does both of these things. It invests in three key areas that look poised for superior growth in the next few years: technology, health care, and financial services. And when you look at the performance of this fund, you see it has a four-star ranking from Morningstar and is ranked in the top 10 percent of its class when compared with similar funds. And the five-year record that I mentioned? It's returned over 20 percent in that period.

A Quick Critique

- His presentation is based on facts, numbers, and opinion (all left-brain tools of logic).
- His presentation puts the onus on the broker's recommendation. The client's buy-in will be based on agreement with the broker's opinion.
- This worn approach can be made regarding a thousand other funds. What does the client remember about the presentation a week later other than, "My broker recommended it?"

Broker #2:

(Before talking, he pulls out a piece of paper and draws a timeline from 1946 to 2008. The clients' eyes follow his pen.)
Mr. and Mrs. Jones, you could get a thousand opinions from a thousand people about what the market will do and where to put your money. But markets always come back to one simple principle—supply and demand. When more people spend more money, profits rise and our investments rise with them.
I drew this timeline to tell you the story about why our markets have done so well in recent years and will continue to do well. This story starts with the GIs coming home from WWII and starting families *(makes a wry smile, then points to the year 1946 on the paper)* and this started the baby boom *(starts drawing curve)*. This boom of babies kept up until 1964 and peaked in 1958. Why is this important? Because people buy things and the more people there are, the more things that are sold.
We reach our peak spending years in our mid-40s to late 40s. That's when we have the most money to spend. Now watch this *(points back to chart)*. When did the first baby boomers reach their mid-40s *(waits for an answer—clients point to early 90s on chart)*? Exactly! And you see that this correlates exactly with our amazing bull market. By the

way, the population curve from 1946 on went the opposite way in Japan and look at what has happened to its markets in the last decade.

Now, as these baby boomers continue to earn and age—7 baby boomers turn 50 every minute—we want to know what they are doing with their money. We know the following:

- They're buying the latest technologies *(writes "technology")*.
- They're investing *(writes "financial services")*.
- As they age, they'll spend more on drugs and health products *(writes "health/drugs" and gives the example of Viagra as a baby boomer drug bonanza)*.

Do you see a correlation with people you know in this age group? *(Client gives an example affirming this trend and broker points back to paper.)*

Well, the good news is that the height of the boomer population won't reach their peak spending years until about 2003 or 2004. And we've just identified where they are putting their money *(points to words on paper)*. They're buying computers and the latest technologies, they're investing in stocks and funds, and they're spending more on drugs and health. What we want to do is invest in a fund that puts our money in these areas. *(Broker pauses and waits for a response.)*

The client asks, "What would be the best fund for that?"

(Broker hands them prospectus.)

This fund uses this strategy and has an excellent track record. A lot of my clients have been very happy with this fund and you can see why when you look at the returns.

Let's compare the deliveries of the two brokers and identify how the story-selling approach achieves greater buy-in and a feeling of security. The deliveries point out the cycle of Thoughts-Emotions-Decision that takes place when we are approached or confronted with information (See Figure 3.1).

THOUGHTS: The presenter chooses, by the selection of material or method, which thought processes are going to be triggered. Will this material trigger defensive logic or will it trigger imagination and closely held beliefs?

EMOTIONS: Emotions begin to stir as people are presented with the material. These emotions can sway back and forth or they can start negatively or positively and heighten in intensity in either direction. The decision will ultimately be based

FIGURE 3.1 Thoughts-Emotions-Decision Chart

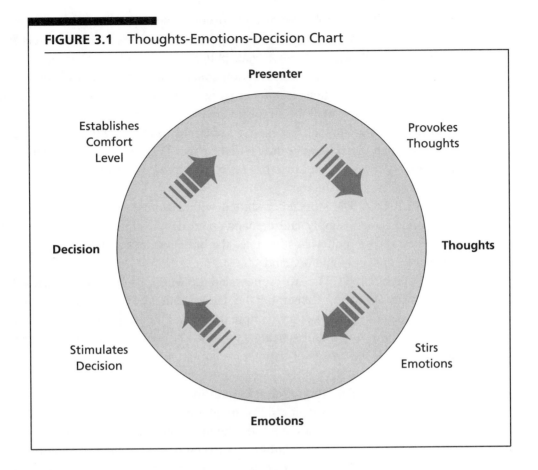

on emotion. This is true even if the clients can't articulate what those emotions are. They feel good or bad, at peace or unsettled, confused or clear, and each feeling will be the rudder that guides the decision ship.

DECISION: The decision will be either go, stop, or wait. People go to other doctors for second opinions because they sense there is something else they need to hear, something their first doctor missed or didn't understand. People will wait and look elsewhere if they don't get the right feeling about what they are hearing from financial professionals. Many of these people turn to financial self-care because they are afraid of being taken advantage of.

CONNECTIONS: Facts, figures, and opinions do very little to form a bond or create a connection between you and your client. When we are dealing strictly with intellectual material we, at best, forge an intellectual connection. When we are dealing with principles, values, philosophy, and experience, we forge a much stronger connection because we are triggering responses at many levels in our clients' thinking: practical, emotional, philosophical, and moral as well as intellectual. The natural result of these plural connections is an increased level of trust in the advisor. Your client is left thinking, "I understood my broker. I learned something. I like the way she simplified matters. I agree with her approach."

VISUAL: The storyseller began without words by drawing a timeline. The clients' eyes and interest were drawn to the page. This stimulates the brain's visual and curiosity triggers. The stage has been set as professor and student are about to enter a market history lesson.

SIMPLICITY: The storyseller started with a simple principle that the clients could understand—supply and demand—and demonstrated how this law would affect their investment. This stimulates the brain's values and beliefs trigger. People believe in supply and demand.

STORYSELLING: The storyseller used the words, "I drew this timeline to tell you the story about . . ." Remember the whole brain is engaged when we announce that we are going to tell a story. Simplicity guided the lesson. Clients can relate to (1) GIs coming home and starting families; (2) boomers earning and spending money; and (3) the effects of boomer spending on certain industries and our markets as a whole.

QUESTIONS: The storyseller asks questions he knows the clients can answer. This draws the students deeper into the lesson, especially when they offer their own examples of this spending trend. The questions create needed pause to check and see if the clients' understanding is keeping pace with the presentation.

FACTS IN SUPPORTING ROLE: The storyseller integrates facts and statistics into the story but does not depend on facts and statistics as a major player in the story. The facts lend credibility and are used as launch points for conclusions.

HUMOR: A touch of light humor keeps the atmosphere relaxed and the interest level high.

LOW PRESSURE: The storyseller's approach is to tell the story and let the clients decide if they want to follow the lessons to be learned from the story. It is her clients' choice. When we present facts and figures and opinions, our clients often feel like they are going along with a decision that was made for them instead of with them.

PRINCIPLES: The story reveals patterns, principles, and a sound philosophy behind the investment strategy. These patterns, principles, and philosophies will appeal emotionally to your clients and work toward allaying deep-seated uncertainties and doubts. Your clients now understand the logic behind the numbers.

They understand the principle—they believe in principle. They see the pattern—they understand this pattern. They agree with the philosophy—they will have a good feeling about the decision. The visual lesson, the storytelling, the simple logic all resulted in greater illumination for the client. Greater illumination leads to peaceful emotions. Peaceful emotions lead to the decision to buy. This is the essence of gut feelings that your clients follow when deciding what to buy and who to buy from.

The second presentation—or the storyselling approach—took more time in delivery, but there were fewer questions about details and doubts after the delivery. Remember that time is relative in the minds of the clients. Two minutes of facts and figures take more psychological time than five minutes of an interesting story. Time flies when they're having fun! Stories, if told well, are intriguing to the client.

The following illustrations reveal how our approach leads to easier decisions for your clients and a more enduring relationship for you (see Figure 3.2).

The generic approach is one where the persuasion method hinges on focusing on facts, figures, and opinions. This focus alone stirs thoughts that lead to emotions of ambivalence and/or skepticism. These statistics look good, but statistics can be misleading and things can change. Most educated people have been taught to keep a skeptical eye on statistics. Intelligent people understand that statistics are easily manipulated.

This, in large part, is what people are getting from their Internet sources: facts, statistics, and opinions. These sources often lead to ambivalence and worse, a false sense of confidence. They need the human factor to find a truly confident course of financial action.

Facts and statistics can easily arouse skepticism. Consider the following that we've heard:

Broker: "This fund has a four-star rating form Morningstar."
Client thought: "Why doesn't it have five stars?"
Broker: "This fund ranked 23 out of 123 in its peer group."
Client thought: "I'd like to see the ones that ranked 1 through 22."
Broker: "This fund has had impressive returns the last three years.
Client thought: "Who hasn't?" Or, "Not as good as the S&P."

Opinions can arouse the same defensiveness as facts and statistics but more passionately so. Most people have taken someone else's opinion in a money matter at some time in their life and have been burned. When people are offered opinions on financial products without knowing the underlying principles and philosophies driving those products, they will usually linger in a state of emotional uncertainty with, "What if they're wrong?" echoing in their mind.

FIGURE 3.2   Generic versus Storyselling Approaches

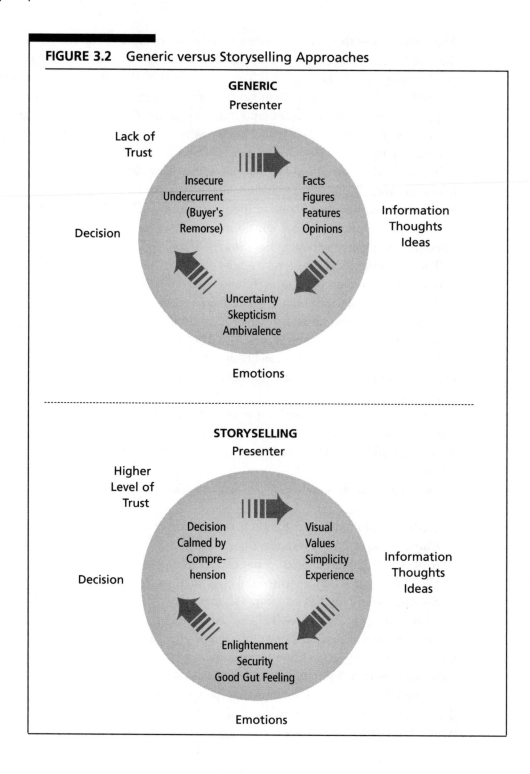

No broker/advisor wants to stir emotions of ambivalence, defensiveness, skepticism, or uncertainty, but many unwittingly do just that by the style of presentation they pursue.

The nature of reasoning or rationale is to stake out a position and then defend it. When we pursue sales approaches that exclusively aim for logic and provoke rationale—while excluding emotion and feeling—we do so to our own peril. Much of the practice of overcoming objections is necessary because the material we used raised those objections in the first place! When we present facts and speculative opinions, they act like a cattle prod to the clients' cerebral system and stir the instantaneous, automatic response to back off and defend.

The double-minded man is unstable in all his ways.

BOOK OF JAMES

Decisions that come out of the generic sales approach are lukewarm at best. The only exception to this is where you and your client have a long-standing relationship and decisions are based more on the relationship (and trust) than on the effectiveness of your presentation. In this case, decisions are based more on relational aspects than on the effectiveness of your presentation. When your clients are given only intellectual fodder to consider when making an investment decision, their mind will work like a see-saw. Their optimistic side will offer logic as to why it will work. Their pessimistic side will offer a rationale for failure and financial catastrophe. After interviewing many clients, we've come to the conclusion that this ambivalence may continue long after the decision to buy. Second-guessing can go on ad infinitum in your clients' minds if you haven't prepared the proper emotional foundation.

I talked to a broker and he showed me a fund that had done well in recent years but lately was down a little. He said this made it a "bargain" and I should seriously consider investing in it. So I did. When I looked it up in the paper, it had gone down even more. I don't see the bargain in that. I mean the numbers looked good and everything, but I just don't understand why it's going nowhere and my friends' funds are doing great.

LARRY D., CLIENT

This sort of second-guessing is second nature to most. However, it is also a symptom of a client who has not been emotionally and intellectually prepared for

I talked to a broker and he showed me a fund that had done well in recent years but lately was down a little. He said this made it a "bargain" and I should seriously consider investing in it. So I did. When I looked it up in the paper, it had gone down even more. I don't see the bargain in that. I mean the numbers looked good and everything, but I just don't understand why it's going nowhere and my friends' funds are doing great.

the inevitable ebb and flow of securities-based funds. Turn on an investment advice radio show and listen to the number of callers asking, "I bought such and such, is that good? What should I do?"

We hear those callers and wonder how good a job their brokers did to help them understand what it was they were investing in. Such clients wouldn't be plagued by second-guessing, and they wouldn't be jamming the lines of talk radio financial gurus if they had the kind of connection with their financial advisors that storyselling can produce.

We don't want your clients to make decisions based on high degrees of uncertainty. Such relationships are transitory because of the insecure undercurrent in your clients' minds. Transitory, short-term relationships are not good for you or your clients.

The Securities Industry Association (SIA) commissioned a study asking customers what they thought of the financial advisors who serve them. These two findings came out of that study:

1. Two-thirds of the investors in the study felt more loyalty to their personal broker than to their brokerage firm.
2. Nearly half of the investors felt their broker could improve his or her services by making a greater effort to educate.

This storyselling approach works to "achieve loyalty through illumination." The light you turn on in their comprehension inspires their confidence in you. You, as a financial advisor, are responsible for making complex issues simple, helping your clients feel informed and knowledgeable, and leaving them with a feeling of calm and illumination. As a result, your clients will begin to feel a resolute sense of loyalty to you.

Storysellers are differentiated from the pack by the thoughts they provoke in the minds of their clients. Remember the Thoughts-Emotions-Decision cycle discussed previously? Brokers provoke thoughts designed to stir emotions that will promote decisions. The presentation process should be designed to make decision making easy. A majority of the time, clients cannot decide "because they just don't understand." They don't understand because their financial advisor did not teach them well. Refer again to Figure 3.2, Generic versus Storyselling Approaches. The chart illustrates, if nothing else, how easy it is for you, the advisor, to separate yourself from the monotonous pack.

Not only is the storyselling approach more effective, it is more fun! It is enjoyable to draw illustrations, tell stories, relate experiences, and connect with the beliefs and hopes of your clients.

Helping your clients to achieve that good gut feeling is your chief aim. Once they feel right, the decision is made. You stir the desired feelings by the thoughts you provoke. The selection of material you'll use to provoke specific thoughts is crucial. If you fail to stir the desired thoughts, the thoughts-emotions-decision cycle will work against you.

If the light of illumination comes on for your client because of a story you told or an analogy you shared, you just made the leap in her mind from broker to financial guru. You became a source for not only advice but for wisdom and understanding as well.

THE THOUGHTS YOU PROVOKE

The watchwords for the thoughts you provoke are descriptive, simple, and experiential. This is why the storyseller uses illustrations to connect with the visual learning center in the right side of the brain. Seventy percent of all learners claim they learn better visually than they do audibly. We ought to take a clue from this.

A study on learning retention once concluded that we retain 11 percent of what we hear, 30 percent of what we see, 50 percent of what we see and hear, and 70 percent of what we do. If this is true, we should strive to make our presentations as multisensory as possible. The more senses we stimulate, the richer the experience will be in the client's memory. Our model begins with provoking thoughts by stimulating many senses from the sense of sight to the sense of humor. We want to use visuals, values, simplicity, and experience.

VISUAL: You want the client to use both the outer and the inner eye. Your illustrations will stimulate the outer eye, your anecdotes and analogies will stimulate the inner eye—the imagination. Visual input triples your impact.

VALUES: Get your clients to start thinking about what their beliefs and principles about their money are. Once they reveal their values or guiding philosophy, it is easier to make recommendations they will be comfortable with.

SIMPLICITY: Simplicity leads to understanding. Understanding leads to a calm emotional state. A calm emotional state leads to positive decisions and a high comfort level in the advisor-client relationship.

EXPERIENCE: People want the tried and true. Even if a company or fund is new, they like knowing that the principles or philosophy for investing have been tried by fire. Your depth of experience leads to greater assurance in their minds. That you've been "around the block" is the feeling and impression you want your clients to have.

HOW DOES IT FEEL?

In storyselling you purposely ask questions, draw illustrations, use analogies, and tell stories for the purpose of stirring target emotions.

When you tap into values, experiences, and hopes and get people to think in terms of pictures, not numbers, the sum result is a calmer emotional state. This is the good gut feeling that every sales presentation should aim to achieve. The decisions clients make are the natural result of the emotional state you help them reach. You guide clients to this emotional state with the thoughts you provoke.

The Thoughts-Emotions-Decision cycle is premised on stirring the right side of the brain where the "risk throttle" and the gut feeling abide. When bombarded with numbers and data, people often grow agitated and tense because their minds' computers must now process these numbers. With pictures, principles, and experiences, however, people become involved and grow reflective. You are now appealing to the movie screen in your client's brain. When you do this you are illuminating your client and greatly increasing the relational glue and potential for permanence in that relationship.

THE IMPOTENCE OF LOGIC

The storyseller understands that emotions are the key to decision making. Logic is highly overrated. Too much emphasis has been placed on the persuasive power of analysis and logic. Logic does not change emotions—perceptions change emotions. This is the reason advertising agencies create perceptions and attach them to products. If you wear these shoes, you are a champion, a winner. If you drink this soda, you are a risk taker living on the edge. Drive this car and you are controlling your own destiny. Perceptions alter emotions. Decisions are based on which way emotions are altered. Logic-based presentations based on fact and analysis put half the brain to sleep and produce negligible impact on emotions.

The storyseller is in the business of creating favorable perceptions. By reducing complex investment issues into simple, understandable, and metaphorical terms, you promote the perception that your clients can understand what they are buying.

PERCEPTION: "This advisor helps me learn. I feel enlightened." Simultaneously you promote the perception that you have such a profound grasp of matters that you can easily and readily describe them in terms any person can understand.

PERCEPTION: "This advisor is a teacher with a deep well of knowledge. I feel I can trust him with my money." You improve your people skills by grasping the personality predisposition of your clients and by making the communication adjustments necessary to forge an optimum personal connection and bond. Your clients now feel comfortable with you and are more willing to trust you.

PERCEPTION: "This advisor understands me. She speaks my language and makes me feel comfortable."

This gut feeling that we all check before deciding on any matter of importance is really our intuition at work. It is the way the right side of our brain makes decisions. The left side of our brain makes decisions by going through a checklist. This process takes lots of time and the left side of the brain is constantly second-guessing itself. The right side of our brain takes in all the information and observations it makes about the person making the presentation and stirs it up like a blender and makes a call—go, no, or wait! We can't always offer a list of logical reasons for the decisions we make. Those decisions are often based on a feeling—and we have learned to follow that instinct.

While we were talking to the advisor, we told him about a particular mutual fund we thought we would like. He said that although he could set us up in the one we mentioned, he would rather see us invest in a different fund. He was aggressive in his recommendation. We knew the commissions were higher on the fund he was recommending. We understood that he has to make a living, but this attitude gave us the feeling that his own financial well-being was being placed above ours. We had been feeling good about him until then, but at that point our trust level really began to drop.

ED AND NANCY, CLIENTS

VAPOR OF PAST EXPERIENCE

A 75-year-old client put it this way, "I know in 30 seconds if this broker is someone I want to work with. I've become very intuitive in my decision making and I can tell in the first 30 seconds if the broker is a shyster or trustworthy—if he's looking out for my best interests or his own."

A 75-year-old client put it this way, "I know in 30 seconds if this broker is someone I want to work with. I've become very intuitive in my decision making and I can tell in the first 30 seconds if the broker is a shyster or trustworthy—if he's looking out for my best interests or his own."

Joyce C. Hall, the founder of Hallmark, once defined intuition as the vapor of past experience. Contrast this vapor with memorized information, which is nothing more than mental noise.

One of the greatest assets we retain is our memory bank. We are constantly comparing what we see and hear with the vapor of our past experiences. By the time we turn 65, our memory storehouse has grown from a closet to a vast warehouse of neatly arranged experiences and memories.

People are comparing what they see in you and what they hear you say with the vapor of their past experiences and arriving at an intuitive decision based on a feeling they got. If your manner reminds them of someone they knew who talked over their head or wasn't a good listener, that association is made in their brains and they'll find someone else that they feel more comfortable with.

I know a woman who was fighting for her life and seeing one of the top oncologists in the world. He was an outstanding researcher and analyst but had poor communication skills. He didn't make eye contact, didn't always speak clearly, and had an air of condescension. Even though her life was hanging in the balance, she wanted to change doctors because of the rotten feeling she got when talking to him. A logical decision? No. Her emotions were swayed by the perception that he really didn't care about her. Again, feelings trump logic in the decision-making process. This is because, for the majority of people, the decision to move, to do, to risk, is an intuitive call coming from the right side of the brain. People trust their own intuitions over any fact or statistic you may show them.

The left side of the brain is the monitor. The right side of the brain is the mover. If you want to see people move the way top producers stimulate them to move, you will have to learn to operate on a more intuitive level.

I once read something by an astronaut who had landed on the moon that in training as an astronaut, 10 percent of the time was spent studying plans for the mission and 90 percent of the time learning to react intuitively to all the "what ifs." That's the same approach I take on my job as an advisor. You can become too reliant on what you know and pay too little attention to responding intuitively to what clients really want to know. They have fears and concerns that I need to pick up on and address. I can't do this if I'm trying to push my way through an agenda.

ERIC L., FINANCIAL ADVISOR

The astronaut that this advisor referred to was Edgar Mitchell, the sixth man on the moon who founded the Institute for Noetic Sciences in California. The term *noetic science* comes from the word *noetre,* which is the eye for intuitive knowing. Mitchell claimed that reliance on the intuitive response was the most important part of the astronauts' training. From what we've observed from highly successful brokers and advisors, *reliance on the intuitive response may also be the most important part of the advisor's job.*

The most powerful intuitive tool any broker/advisor possesses for making a connection with their clients is the incisive, insightful question. Ask the right questions and people will reveal everything you need to know to calm their fears, dispel their confusion, and simplify their life.

Storysellers ask before they tell. Storysellers understand that the most powerful story that can be told is one they cajole their clients to tell. Asking incisive questions is the topic of Chapter 5, "How Socrates Can Help You Reach Your Sales Quota."

To summarize the storyseller's approach: *Decisions get made when the right emotions are stirred (calm, security, trust).* These emotions are stirred through the use of simple visuals and metaphors, sharing of experiences, and addressing values. Storysellers keep their presentations simple, stir the right emotions, respect individuality, and earn trust by both their teaching skills and people skills.

In storyselling

- facts and figures are presented in a visual way;
- values are discovered before features are disclosed; and
- experiences are shared instead of opinions offered.

So if you knew there was a simple way to help people feel illuminated by you as an advisor and comfortable with you as a person, why would you continue to deluge people with the same old boring and confusing materials and presentations that every other advisor is using?

Good question.

WHAT MY BRAIN TELLS ME ABOUT YOU

Helping a customer achieve a good gut feeling about investment products, ideas, and advice is only half the battle in helping clients achieve a secure emotional state. The other half has to do with what the clients' intuitive senses are telling them about you, the advisor. We put our clients in a halfway house of ambivalence if we give them a good feeling about what we know but a queasy feeling about who we are. Perceptions are paramount. Good brokers often unwittingly send negative signals in their body language, tone, manner, and choice of language. The next chapter will focus on how to effect positive signals in these four areas and what to do and what to avoid to allay clients' fears and stir calm and assured emotions.

PART TWO

Becoming a Better Storyseller

4 | Reading and Leading Others: The 30-Second Body Language Read

I once saw a survey that asked people what they noted most when others were talking to them. The respondents said something like: 45 percent—body language; 35 percent—tone of voice; and 20 percent—content. It struck a note with me. All I had ever thought about was content, but I started working on sending positive signals with my body language and tone. It seemed that immediately people started warming up to me more quickly. I'm sure I must have been doing things before I was unaware of that were keeping some people at arms length.

CHUCK Z., ADVISOR

In the right side of our brain we possess the ability to read people. Some are more in tune with this ability than others. Some call it gut instinct and some call it a "feeling" about people. What "it" is, is intuitive knowledge of people. Our brain is observing small movements in the face, eyes, hands, and posture and processing the pace and cadence of speech. This information is thrown into the brain and the right-side intelligence throws back a spontaneous good or bad feeling about the person we are observing.

While the judgment center in the left side of the head works like a calculator, adding and subtracting assets and liabilities one at a time, the judgment coming from the right side acts like a blender, gathers information quickly and instinctively, whirs it all together, and emotes a feeling or sense about the individual in question.

Ask people why they don't feel right about an individual and they can't always articulate the logic behind this feeling. They will follow this ineffable feeling even in the absence of reasoning to support it. Later, they may see or hear something about the individual in question that affirms their spontaneous judgment.

"I couldn't quite put my finger on it," we've heard people say, "but there was something in their manner that bothered me." What these people are experiencing is the intuitive voice in the right side of their brain throwing up a yellow caution flag.

There are two areas of body language an advisor needs to know: (1) how to send positive signals to the client and (2) how to read hesitant signals from the client.

THE SIGNALS YOU SEND

Women speak two languages, one of which is verbal.

STEVE REUBENSTEIN

In important presentations we must learn to be conscious of the fact that many of the body language signals that we send are automatic—that is, we don't think about sending the signal, it just happens. The emotion senses an instantaneous motor response. Some examples: when angry we tense our lips; when doubting, we raise our eyebrows; when disgusted, we wrinkle our noses; when we find someone or something incredulous, we roll our eyes. The eyes and the face have a language of their own. We send numerous unintended and misinterpreted signals to people each day.

My wife and children often ask, "Are you mad?" because of my habit of pursing my lips and narrowing my eyes when I'm concentrating on a thought. It makes me wonder how many times I've given an unintended message to a client or coworker with my unintended facial language.

Successful brokers/advisors wouldn't think of going into a presentation without rehearsing their content, yet surveys indicate that people are swayed or influenced more by body language than by content. Why don't we go through a quick rehearsal of our body language as well? The best persuaders make a practice of projecting specific messages through their body language. After some practice the warm, relaxed, and positive language becomes automatic in these sessions.

If you're truly interested in finding out what you are currently projecting in your eyes, face, and physical manner, ask your associates or family members—the ones who will speak with candor!

Check Yourself

- ❏ Your eyes—Are your eyes open, receptive, and inviting or questioning, intense, and scrutinizing?
- ❏ Your facial muscles—Are your facial muscles tense (communicating disapproval, stress) or are they relaxed? Can you smile easily with your teeth and eyes?
- ❏ Hands—Are your hands closed? Are you pointing? Are your hands open (communicating generosity, helpfulness, and open-mindeness) and your gestures smooth and gentle?
- ❏ Posture—Are you looking down your nose? Are you too far or too close? Is your posture open or closed?

When the eyes say one thing and the tongue another, a practiced man relies on the language of the first.

RALPH WALDO EMERSON

Check Your Client: Warning Signs

- ❏ The raised eyebrow—Needs validation, shows pessimism
- ❏ Scrunched-up nose—Lacks credibility, foolish
- ❏ Narrowed eyes—Uncertain, skeptical
- ❏ Rolling eyes and/or pursed lips—Shows disapproval, disgust
- ❏ Frozen smile—Afraid to express true feelings of disapproval or disagreement
- ❏ Nervous gestures—Anxious about topic at hand or just a constant nervous habit (e.g., tapping fingers, shuffling objects)
- ❏ Darting/fidgeting eyes—Bored; feels pace too slow or material irrelevant
- ❏ Hand to forehead—Confused or stressed
- ❏ Hand to chin—Processing the information
- ❏ Looking away—Avoiding topic or conflict
- ❏ Looking up—Thinking through topic
- ❏ Head on desk; loud snoring sound—Presentation so good you put them in a dream state!

We have seen many advisors fail to yield to or comprehend these physical gestures and as a result "drive right through the signal." The wise thing to do is to show as much vigilance toward body language as to spoken language. People are rarely comfortable saying, "I'm confused," "I'm skeptical," "I disapprove," "You lack credibility," or "This is wrong." However, the body and face deliver automatic responses. Most people can't control these automatic responses. Only the most skilled negotiators and poker players are adept at masking the automatic facial tics of body language.

Each client meeting is a negotiation. *The skilled negotiator understands the need to read and heed signals from the client that it is to time to stop, to yield, or to turn around.*

Look for automatic facial and physical signals, yield, clarify, and then move down your presentation path—if indeed that is where the client wants to go.

If you choose to ignore these signals, don't be surprised when you find you've lost your passenger!

EYES ARE THE GATEWAY TO THE SOUL

Whether you believe it is superstition or science, people put a lot of stock in what they perceive from their eyes. A personality course called TEAM Dynamics instructs people how to read an individual's personality type by looking into their eyes. The four basic personality types are Togetherness, Enterpriser, Analyzer, and Motivator. Each personality style possesses a unique and discernible eye language. (See Figure 4.1.)

The Togetherness personality's eyes send the message, "I am amicable, interested, and sincere. I'm a good listener and I care about others." The Enterpriser's eyes send this message: "I am driven, I am confident, and I get the job done." The Analyzer's eyes send the message, "I'm not too sure, I'm thinking about it. I have some questions," The Motivator's eyes send the message, "I'm enjoying life, seizing the moment, and having fun!"

One or two of these personalities are dominant in most of us, and our eyes are the window to what these dominant styles are. We all possess a degree of each of these four styles of personality, but one or two of the styles dominate in the majority of us. About 15 to 20 percent of the people you meet show a balance in all four styles and are difficult to read in terms of body language because of the mixed signals they send.

The majority of people you meet (80 to 85 percent) give very clear facial, tonal, and posture signals that are dead giveaways of their personal style. The keys to knowing what and what not to say to each of these styles is revealed in the first

FIGURE 4.1 Team Dynamics—Body Language Clues to Personality

	Togetherness	Enterpriser	Analyzer	Motivator
Eyes	• Soft/Caring • Interested	• Laser • Busy	• Scanning • Scrutinizing • Intense	• Open • Happy • Dancing
Face	• Pleasant/ Reserved smile • Assuring head nods	• Exudes confidence • Smirking • Defiant	• Nonanimated (Poker face) • Can appear disapproving	• Big smile (lots of teeth) • Animated
Posture	• Blushes easily • Nonthreatening • Conforming	• Take charge ("I'm the boss") • Power	• Rigid • Reserved • Controlled	• Free- flowing • Relaxed
Physical Style	Steady, plodding	Fast, fidgety	Slow, meticulous	Fast, random
Voice	• Constant, steady tone • Constantly affirming (Fre- quently says "OK" and "I see")	• Punctuated • Emphatic • Candid speech	• Monotone • Hesitates before responding	• Laughs easily • Full range of pitches • Talks loud and fast
Key Phrase	"What do you think?"	"Just do it."	"I need to know . . ."	"Let's party!"

minute you meet the individual—in the eyes, the face, the tone, and the posture. I always look to the eyes first because I've found that 75 percent of the time I can get an accurate read from my initial look into eyes.

The eyes reveal the personality.

Once you understand what personality you're dealing with, you know exactly which route to take in your presentation for optimum connection with your client. This is called the TEAM Dynamic. A TEAM Dynamic means clients feel their advisor is connecting with their style and is working with them—not working on them.

One investment firm I worked with started using this program for their financial advisors who sold 403(b) plans to teachers after they discovered that most of their brokers were polar opposites of the majority of their teacher clients. The brokers were Enterpriser/Motivator personalities and the majority of the teachers were Togetherness/Analytical personalities.

By learning to recognize body and tonal signals, these advisors were able to adjust their communication style and pace to a style that was more comfortable to their clients.

How should this knowledge of your clients' personalities affect your approach and delivery? In every way imaginable! If you know their personalities, it should affect how you greet them, how much small talk you engage in, and what small talk topics you discuss. It should affect the pace and content of your presentation and how you follow up.

For example, each of these personality styles prefers a different twist in your presentation. If you can spot this and deliver the angle each prefers, your clients are going to get a good feeling about you, thereby greatly increasing your chances of retaining them. Here are the angles that the four personalities prefer:

The Togetherness personality. The Togetherness personality asks "how" questions. For example, "How does this relationship work?" or "How do these investments work?" or "How do I know if I'm doing things right?"

The Togetherness personality has a great need for a step-by-step breakdown and for affirmation. This personality looks for sincerity, consistency, and commitment, wants to be asked questions, and wants to be led gently.

When dealing with a Togetherness personality, keep these ten points in mind:

1. Use inclusive language like, "*Our* plan will be . . ." and "What *we* need to do is . . ."
2. Use a supportive approach. "Here's what we'll do for you after today's meeting . . ."
3. Use statements of commitment. "We view this as a life-time commitment— that's why we develop only long-term plans."
4. Explain the broad picture in steps. "Let me break our strategy down into these four steps . . ."
5. Express sincere interest in your clients.
6. Slow down the pace and don't rush your clients.
7. Project a listening, respective posture toward your clients.
8. Do not present in a condescending, autocratic, or authoritarian manner.
9. Help your clients deal with their fears.
10. Allow your clients time to make their own decisions.

The Enterpriser personality. The Enterpriser personality is the exact opposite of the Togetherness personality. Where the Togetherness personality is feeling oriented, the Enterpriser is results oriented.

The Enterpriser personality asks "what" and "why" questions. For example, "What's the bottom line?" or "What are you going to make from this?" or "Why do I need that?"

The Enterpriser personality is take-charge, confrontational, candid, and competitive. It has a strong ego and doesn't like being told what to do. Enterprisers often lack patience and grow angry when things are started and not finished. Enterprisers know how to get things done and want to see that same competency in you!

When dealing with the Enterpriser personality, follow these ten key points:

1. Get to the point. "I'm already two pages ahead of you!"
2. Don't bore your client with details.
3. Don't insult your client with corny jokes or long, boring stories.
4. Ask your client's opinion first and offer yours later.
5. Respect your client's time.
6. Show your client the big picture right away.
7. Use concise statements containing only relevant information.
8. Show your client the possibilities.
9. Don't tell your client what to do unless you're asked.
10. Speak plainly: your client probably has a good BS detector!

The Analyzer personality. The Analyzer is a plodding, pensive, and rational personality that demands detail. Analyzers have high standards for themselves and others. They are skeptical and often pessimistic in their thinking. They do not like being pushed or hurried.

The Analyzer personality asks "what," "why," and "how" questions. For example, "How do I know this is the best deal?" or "What if it doesn't work as projected?" or "Why did you select that company's funds?" or the oft-heard Analyzer refrain, "How can you prove that?"

Use these ten key points:

1. Don't expect your client to make big decisions with small amounts of information.
2. Don't make claims or promises that you can't prove or fulfill.
3. Slow down the pace and allow your client time to decide.

4. Don't say, "I know you will like this."
5. Provide data and documentation.
6. Don't try to convince your client with emotion, "schmoozing," or excitement.
7. Use flawless logic to persuade your client.
8. Display patience when meeting your client's need for documentation and proof.
9. Be studious, prepared, and organized.
10. Give equal explanation to risks as well as rewards.

The Motivator personality. The Motivator is the exact opposite of the Analyzer. Where Analyzers are logical, thorough, and detailed, Motivators are more emotional and impulsive and abhor detail. The Motivator is persuaded by dialogue, fellowship, having a good time, and a sense that you are a "good Joe." Motivators like to talk but they'll listen to your advice. They don't want to be bogged down with detail and would rather delegate the entire matter to someone else.

The Motivator personality likes to ask "who" questions. For example, "Who are some of your other clients in town here?" (fishing for VIPs) or "Who runs this fund you are talking about?" or "Who in my circle do you know?"

Follow these ten tips for working with Motivators:

1. Provide a relaxed and casual atmosphere.
2. Take the time to "chew the fat" and get to know your client.
3. Do not be afraid to jump off course during your presentation.
4. Smile.
5. Use a quick pace and keep it interesting.
6. Show enthusiasm and have a sense of humor.
7. Provide testimonials.
8. Plant seeds of information only and avoid the use of small print and thick piles of information.
9. Provide your clients with opportunities to verbalize their goals and optimism.
10. Provide a plan that supports your clients' dreams.

Remember, the good gut feeling that we want to stimulate with each and every client is the result of two separate understandings: (1) how well you understand the topic and how good you are at educating your client; and (2) how well you understand your client's personality and how good you are at connecting with the client's style.

The people skills we are discussing here are tantamount in importance to your analytical and advisory skills. If you can excel at both you will never want for clients.

Far too many professionals think they can get by on professional competence alone. The storyseller realizes that understanding the person he or she is dealing with is just as important as understanding the topic of investments. This is true because people buy based on emotion. They are directed by a gut feeling, which is really the intuitive voice saying, "Go!" or "No!" With these body language reading and communication skills, you will soon become expert at both reading and leading your clients.

5 How Socrates Can Help You Reach Your Sales Quota

Getting Others to Tell Their Story

It takes reason to answer a question well. It takes imagination to ask it well.

ANONYMOUS

Questions are the creative acts of intelligence.

FRANK KING

How many times in your career of selling have you gone out and fired a perfect bullseye in your presentation only to find it was your target you hit and not your client's? How many times have you climbed the ladder of success only to find it was leaning against the wrong wall? We've all been there and done that.

The greatest mistake we make in selling is neglecting to learn more about our customers before making our presentation. We are so excited or passionate about telling our story that we fail to hear our clients' stories.

Remember the broker-client clock we talked about in Chapter 2? Forty-nine seconds out of every 60 the broker does the talking. Is our presentation so important that it should dominate 82 percent of the air time in our client meetings? The only way a person can excel by dominating 82 percent of the clock is to possess a

> **Q**uestions are the creative acts of intelligence.

psychic gift. Do brokers have an extra sensory perception (ESP) that tells them what their client thinks and feels? This ESP gift also provides a broker with all clients' background and experience, ups and downs, values, and hopes regarding their money. Do brokers possess supernatural mind-reading abilities so that it is only necessary to allow a client 11 seconds out of every minute to talk? Eleven seconds! That's barely enough time to ask where the bathroom is!

This 49-11-second broker-client communication statistic violates some very basic rules of human relations, not to mention the laws of intelligent selling. These rules:

- The more time you spend learning about the experiences and views of your clients, the more weight they will give to *your* experience and views. This truth is so simple that most sales professionals completely ignore it—all except the very best, that is.
- If you don't ask before you tell, you have no assurance that you are telling what the client is asking for. How can you be sure you are on the bullseye when you've taken no time to let the client define the target?

Even though almost every sales training program emphasizes the need to listen more skillfully, sales professionals persist in wanting to talk, dominating conversations. As one client put it, "Some sales professionals seem to be simply in love with the sound of their own voice."

Rather than being a course on how to become a better listener, this chapter is a course on how to ask better questions. Ask the right questions and people will talk. You have to possess only enough sense to be attentive and look for the clues you'll need to forge a connection. Critical emotions, experiences, values, and hopes are revealed when you ask the right questions. There is a relational payoff. Once you ask

- you'll understand what makes your clients tick, what they can and can't tolerate, the highly charged emotional issues to avoid, and the principles you can use to forge a bond (we call this "discovering land mines and gold mines"); and
- you'll find your clients appreciate your asking—they're impressed that you're interested in them as individuals, not just as accounts.

Framing the Picture You're about to Paint

According to sales training expert Gary DeMoss, questions you ask act as a framework for the picture you will paint in your presentation. (See Figure 5.1.) Great presentations are works of art. They require creativity and inspiration. On the other hand, building a frame is a constructive task. It is a process of precise query and workmanship. The questions in this chapter will help you to discover key aspects of your clients' life, work, values, and expectations of you as a broker.

FIGURE 5.1 Framing the Picture You're about to Paint

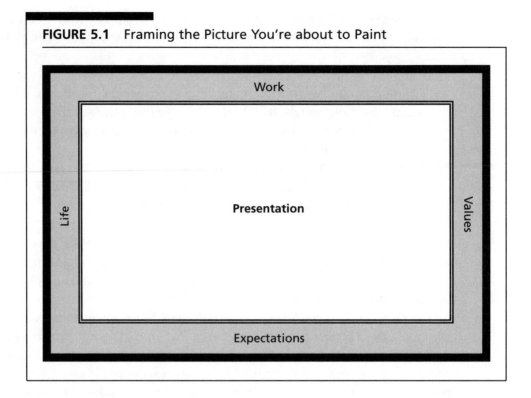

THE SOCRATIC SELL

Never lead with statements when you could lead with questions.

SOCRATES (AUTHOR'S PARAPHRASE)

Maybe you've seen the parlor trick in which you write down the three of hearts on a piece of paper, fold it up, and put it in your pocket. You then pick a member of your audience and tell him or her that you'd like to talk about a deck of cards. You begin by saying, "Now you're aware that there are four suits in a deck; name any two." If the individual says, "Hearts and diamonds," you say, "And out of those two name one." If the response is "Hearts," you say, "OK, so the suit you've selected is . . . ?" He or she answers, "Hearts."

You say, "OK, write that down. Now, let's move on to numbers."

But if at the beginning the individual states, "Spades and clubs," you say, "O.K., and which two suits did you leave out?" He or she will answer, "Hearts and diamonds." You reply, "Hearts and diamonds—and out of those two, name one."

If the response is, "Diamonds," you say, "And the suit you just left out was . . . ?" The response is, "Hearts." You say, "So the last suit you mentioned was . . . hearts? OK, write that down. Now, let's move on to numbers."

In this game you use the same process of questions and elimination until the individual arrives at the three of hearts. The fun of the trick is that, because of your technique, the participants think they have come up with the three of hearts on their own, and they are mystified when you pull the paper out of your pocket with the three of hearts.

This little mind game is an intriguing introduction to the concept of the *Socratic sell*. The larger lesson here is that anywhere you can lead by telling, you can lead to the same place more efficiently by asking. You should never tell when you can ask.

In the card trick, we're using the method as a manipulation to get someone to choose what we've already chosen for them. In doing so, we've made them feel that it was their choice. There are times when such manipulations are appropriate—for example, when we want our children to make a certain choice that we know is best for them. There have possibly been certain selling situations you've been in where you knew exactly what your clients needed but knew if you told them they would reject your advice because of ego, stubbornness, or misconception. Probably in those situations you have employed this technique of well-thought-out questions to allow the clients to talk themselves into the very thing you had to offer.

Manipulation is a word that carries a stigma in our society and is used most frequently to describe negative coercion and control. Manipulation, however, is a neutral term that means "to move or influence in one direction or another." If we are using our powers of persuasion to coax an individual into doing something that will benefit his or her life, we are still manipulating. Because our aim was noble and our motives pure, our persuasion is usually referred to as good influence rather than manipulation.

It is not the manipulation potential of intelligent questioning that we wish to focus on with the Socratic approach but the larger lesson that *the most profound method of persuasion is found in asking intelligent questions.* We have observed that those advisors who have developed the skill of asking intelligent, incisive questions also possess superior skills in giving intelligent answers.

However, the opposite is not always true. Many professionals who can offer intelligent answers quite often ask foolish questions or worse, no questions at all. Those who ask very few questions operate purely on assumptions—a dangerous game for anyone in sales!

DIGGING FOR GOLD

Individuals who ask intelligent questions are better thinkers. Intelligent inquiry is like mining. You are digging for gold. You are scraping the walls of the client's mind and memory and looking for veins with which you can connect. But intelligent inquiry's payoff is much more far-reaching than just the dividends of gathering information about a client's life. Intelligent inquiry results in manifold relational rewards:

- People like being asked.
- People like to talk about their life.
- People respect you for asking.
- People feel more important because you asked.

Classic sales training breaks the sales process into three categories: discovery, presentation, and close (or advance). For some reason, whether it's impatience or imprudence, many sales professionals pay token observance to the discovery process and put all their chips on their ability to wow the client with their presentation. Yet the close rate hinges more on the discovery process than it does on the power of the presentation. It is in the discovery process that we ascertain whether the client has a proper fit with our product. It is in the discovery process that we do the reconnaissance work that ensures that our delivery is zeroed in on the client's most pulsating need.

I was riding next to a wealthy old woman on an airplane and we got to talking about investments. With a great amount of animation and disgust, she said to me, "I've switched all my investment accounts from my broker—I'm so upset with him!"

"Why? What did he do?" I asked.

"Well, he suggested to me that we invest a large portion of money in the Japanese market because it is selling at a bargain price," she said.

"Probably not a real bad idea," I offered.

"Well," she huffed, "if my broker would have bothered to ask, I would have told him that I lost my beloved husband in the Pacific in World War II. He was killed by a Japanese bomb. And I'll be damned if I'm going to invest one penny in the enemy!"

This true story is not as uncommon as you might expect. Hearing it begs some questions: How long did her broker know her? How long had he been managing her investments? Why had he not bothered to spend a little time learning more about her past? In this particular discovery, negligence led to a loss of business. In many other presentations, a lack of discovery leads to never landing the account in the first place.

Many clients have the attitude, "If you don't ask, I'm not going to tell." The underlying attitude behind this is, "I am worth knowing, but you'll have to show sufficient interest" or, as one individual client told us, "If you're not interested enough in me or my life, why should I bother casting my pearls before the swine?"

Storyseller's axiom: Your level of inquiry reveals your level of interest in the client.

If you don't invest in sufficient discovery, you appear to be more interested in pushing a product than you are in helping your client.

The most outstanding and recurring common denominator we observed in top advisors is the well-developed art of framing provocative and incisive questions. And the brokers are skilled listeners as well. The clients seem to tacitly record the sincere, genuine interest these brokers/advisors are demonstrating. More than the gift of gab, these advisors all had the innate ability to get others to talk. While they are listening, these advisors are intuitively putting together the pieces of the puzzle that will become a client's investment picture.

> **I**f you don't invest in sufficient discovery, you appear to be more interested in pushing a product than you are in helping your client.

We have observed some people remarkably skilled in getting others to talk. One example is Larry, who has led his company in sales for seven consecutive years. The strange thing about watching Larry sell is that he never seems to be selling. He loves to ask clients about their background and journey to the present. He asks questions like, "How did your business get started?" which would open the door to an interesting autobiographical account of the client's aspirations and tribulations.

As the client talks, Larry starts picking up on patterns, key emotional issues, attitudes, and, most important, fears. Larry has mastered the art of honing in on the fears, uncertainties, and doubts, or FUD, as he likes to call it. He operates on the philosophy that people are more motivated by consequences than benefits. People are moved to action more by the thought of losing something than they are by the thought of gaining something, or as Larry asked, "How many converts would the preacher get if he couldn't talk about hell?"

Once Larry had intuitively deciphered the controlling fear or insecurity the client is battling with, he simply and subtly addressed it with statements like: "If you want to simplify your affairs, a good move would be . . ." or "If you want to be able to sleep at night knowing what you've worked for is secure, you could . . ."

The key to Larry's outstanding sales success was discovering the fear, uncertainty, and doubt that would move the client to action and then offering a salutary proposal to answer those fears and uncertainties.

Cut to the quick or get to the core are the instinctive mottoes that guide top advisors in the discovery process. The Socratic approach is a persuasion philosophy that recognizes these key truths that top advisors practice:

- I never learn a thing while my mouth is moving.
- Ask the right questions and people will tell you what to sell them and how to sell it.
- If you don't have what they need, tell them.

Is it a coincidence that highly successful brokers are wise inquirers and genuinely interested listeners? Is it a coincidence that they are more interested in meeting a client's need than pushing a particular product? Hardly. Their thinking is not limited to meeting sales quotas and minimum acceptable standards. As one broker put it, "I've made a lot of money following the golden rule."

Kay Shirley, who runs a highly successful investment firm in Atlanta and is the author of *The Baby Boomer's Financial Wake-up Call,* guides her clients with this guiding principle: I will sell no product to my clients that I do not own myself.

COAXING CLIENTS TO REVEAL THEIR BIOGRAPHIES

Every man is, in certain respects, (A) . . . like all men, (B) . . . like some other men, (C) . . . like no other man."

C. KLUCKHOLM AND H. MURRAY

Who are these individuals sitting across from you? Just another retired couple, another baby boomer, another widow, another teacher, another business owner? In some respects they are similar to every other person in their classification and demographic. They share similar career backgrounds, similar hopes, similar desires, and similar fears. However, it is a mistake to assume that you know all you need to know based on their careers or stations in life. All humans want to be recognized for their uniqueness. This is especially true in a highly depersonalized age where we are typically identified by a series of ID numbers and account codes. The more you know about each individual's path to the present, the higher his or her comfort level is going to be with you.

I've made it a point to always learn as much as possible about my clients' back-grounds—where they grew up, their career paths, their children, their travels. My reason for this is that I found early in my career that I was often fooled by appearances. I fell into a pattern of judging the book by its cover. Until I started asking, I had no way of knowing that the cosmopolitan-looking woman sitting before me had grown up on a farm, that the simple man with the tacky clothes had traveled around the world, that the average-looking craftsman had once been a world-class athlete. Once I knew those things about them, I had a greater appreciation for them as individuals, and they seemed to reciprocate that appreciation.

GIL A., BROKER

While interviewing and observing top advisors, we were intrigued with the sagacious methods of discovery some of these people used. We have organized the best questions we found into the LIFE Discovery Model. The LIFE (Life Inventory of Formulative Experiences) Discovery Model asks the questions that we found stimulated clients to talk and reveal telling emotions, values, and hopes that they held dear:

- Where are you from?
- Tell me about your work (or the work you did).
- What is the best financial decision you have made in your life?
- Is there anyone besides yourself whose future hinges on your financial decisions?
- Are there any stocks or companies that you would not care to invest in as a matter of principle or for moral reasons?

Question #1: Where Are You From?

An exceptional broker specializing in the 65+ age group told us he always led with this question (it works as well with clients of any age). This broker would get up from his chair and go to a map of the United States on his wall and place a pin on the place the client mentioned. Often, this would get the conversation rolling.

The broker found that when he asked his clients where they were from, their eyes lit up, a fond and nostalgic grin would break out on their faces, and they

The broker found that when he asked his clients where they were from, their eyes lit up, a fond and nostalgic grin would break out on their faces, and they seemed to be instantly transported back to the old town, their childhood, and the home in which they grew up.

seemed to be instantly transported back to the old town, their childhood, and the home in which they grew up. They seemed to relish this opportunity to retrieve sacred souvenirs from their past.

Clients talked about what it was like in those days and how things have changed. They talked about their parents, their siblings, their friends, their activities, their schools, their hangouts, their first jobs, their parents' work and roles, and the "passport" that led them away from that place. "Where are you from?" was the catalyst for an autobiographical stroll down memory lane. What does this question have to do with investment issues? Nothing. What does it have to do with the investor? Everything. *The responses you hear will reveal bedrock values, beliefs, priorities, and dreams these clients hold dear.*

When a retired engineer and his wife were asked where they were from, they were suddenly all smiles and stories. The stress and tension of financial decisions was temporarily lifted. They started speaking of the old New England town where they grew up, how they first met, and where they went from there.

Frank, the conservative and pensive engineer, suddenly had to tell a story. It was about the folks in the old town that knew him. His nickname was Hots. He seemed to take great relish in this nickname as it was a total paradox to his natural modesty and upstanding character. It turns out the nickname was rooted in innocent origins.

Frank described how, when he was 16 years old, he was taking driver's education and the teacher told him to accelerate. Frank hit the gas a little too heavily and spun the tires on the road. The next day the teacher told the class and dubbed him Hots because of the way the tires heated up. Fifty years later, the nickname had stuck and his wife frequently addresses him as Hots.

One of the marvels of hearing a client tell such a story is the transfiguration in the person's demeanor. People don't anticipate going to a broker's office as a fun, engaging experience. While it's not comparable to visiting a dentist or an undertaker, it's not a walk in the park either. Money issues inherently have a degree of stress attached. Getting clients to tell stories about their past acts as a diffuser of that stress.

This relaxing of the environment is but a peripheral benefit of the LIFE Discovery process—but a significant relational benefit at that. The advisor who can instigate storytelling, self-disclosure, nostalgia, and humorous personal insights erects a foundational framework for bridging the chasm of distrust that haunts many clients. Disarming questions result in less defensiveness in the client. And consequently less defensive client meetings.

The primary payoff we observed with this question was the revelation of personal and family heritage and bedrock values. If you want to help people get to where they are going, you need to find out where they have come from. The question about a client's origin helps to decipher what is important to the client, what was important to the client's family, and what the client's dreams and hopes are.

Another profound benefit of the question, "Where are you from?" is that as you are coaxing your clients to provide an autobiographical account, they are revealing to you areas that could have become lethal landmines to your subsequent presentation—for example, the woman who lost her husband in the Pacific and didn't want to invest in Asian stocks.

Brokers and advisors have shared with us many such scenarios, including:

- The client who was downsized by a corporation that the broker had planned on recommending
- The client who, after an accident, had a traumatic experience with an HMO that happened to be a favorite of the advisor
- The client who lost a loved one due to a manufacturing error caused by a well-known transportation company
- The client who had seen a family inheritance rip his family apart in the past and wanted to avoid a similar scenario in the future

Such stories rise to the surface in the course of inquiry into clients' pasts. A litany of traumatic life events are revealed that, if the broker is not aware, can easily lead to clients' quick emotional exodus from the presentation. There are potent emotional issues and life-altering traumas in every person's life. It is your job to find out what those events are before you stick your foot in your mouth or, worse, step on a visceral landmine.

The following story illustrates the consequences of failing to ask a life inventory question before presenting a product:

An insurance agent sat down with my wife and me and began to tell us that a major motivator for purchasing a life insurance/investment policy should be to provide for our children's college education. We thought it was rather presumptuous of this fellow to tell us what our motivations should be rather than ask us how we felt about funding our children's education. Both my wife and I had worked our way through school with negligible aid from our parents. We had discussed this issue and felt the experience had helped to fortify our work ethic and mold our character; and we both had seen too many of our classmates on a free ride from their parents fritter and party away their opportunity to learn. We had decided that our children would (1) earn money toward college; (2) receive matching funds from us based on their earnings; and (3) take out a student loan for the shortfall. Had the insurance broker bothered to ask, we would have explained our philosophy.

He didn't get our business.

The next agent that visited us started by asking the story of our life. That was the best move he could have made. What he discovered was that my wife had lost her first husband to cancer after six months of marriage when she was just 21 years old. Before he died, he had forgotten to sign a document that would have reassigned the benefit on his life insurance policy from his parents to his wife. For some unimaginable and unforgivable reasons, his parents kept the benefit after his death, leaving his widow both bereft and broke.

Consequently, my wife had a morbid fear of another complication in her support should I precede her in death. With the way she felt, no amount of life insurance was enough.

Because he bothered to ask, that agent got the sale.

Asking, "Where are you from?" may sound a tad superfluous at first glance, but when asked with proper intent and with the genuine curiosity of a sleuth, the answers it evokes pay rich dividends to the broker-client relationship. It certainly does more good than banal and prosaic patter about the weather.

The broker's first interest should not be the value of the portfolio but the values that created the portfolio.

Question #2: Tell Me about Your Work or the Work You Did

I asked this older gentleman what he did for a living. He launched into his life story and what a fascinating story it was. It seems this guy was drafted into World War II.

He entered the air force already accomplished as a pilot but didn't get priority as a pilot because he hadn't been trained by the U.S. government. As silly as it sounds, the policy was that you had to be trained by the government to fly for it. Consequently, when he got out of the service, he didn't have as many combat flying hours as other pilots and was passed over by the major airlines because they took pilots with the most combat flying experience. He ended working as a contract pilot his entire life and said he didn't make the kind of money he could have because of the government's policy.

I don't know how true all this was or if it was merely his excuse, but to him it was the central story of his life. He felt victimized by an illogical policy. He told the story with great passion. I agreed with him how ridiculous it was for the government not to use a man's talents simply because they didn't train him.

I then shifted gears and tied the value fund I was selling to his story. I told him it seems that many people want to ignore everything advisors like me had learned in the past 30 years about investing—namely, that a company should be valued based on earnings, growth rates, and managerial experience, which create an underlying value as a business. "Such logic," I said, "seems to be ignored today. The market is in many ways going against common sense."

We made a connection there. He became my client and I think it's because he felt I understood the emotional theme that had run through his life.

Many people derive a major portion of their identity from the work they do or in the work they did. This is a pronounced fact of life. In many cases, if you fail to query your clients on their occupational history, you miss a significant opportunity for a relational connection. Some people identify so strongly with what they do that they need to talk about it. They need to explain, to remember, or even gloat. It's a big part of who they are. They may have an ego need to have others respect or acknowledge their accomplishments. Be especially attuned to this need when you see a lot of alphabet soup after a name; for example, John Q. Genius, M.D., Ph.D., J.D., W.I.I.F.M.

How Did They Get What They Have?

Before I start managing a client's assets, I want to gain a healthy sense of respect for how the client came by his or her money. How many years did it take to gather? What kinds of risks did the client take? Where did the client start? I have heard many stories from people who now live in a palace, but who started in a mobile home. They love telling the story and I love hearing it. I want to know about the blood, sweat, and tears behind the money I'm about to manage. This helps my attitude and my sense of purpose.

FRED K., ADVISOR

Before you start trying to guide your clients' financial future, find out how they gathered the assets they are entrusting to you. Not only does it give you a healthy sense of respect, it helps your clients feel a sense of progress and building. It allows them an emotional pat on the back.

After I ask about the work they did or do, I often follow with, "How did you gather the wealth you've got?" The client often seems flattered and elevated a bit by use of the word wealth. *Many of these people have never thought of themselves as being truly wealthy. I want them to think that way, to see themselves as affluent, because compared with some people, they are! I want them to practice the financial habits that wealthy people practice.*

ALEX B., BROKER

Question #3: What Is the Best Financial Decision You Have Made in Your Life?

Asking clients about their best financial decision gives them a chance to gloat in a personal victory. We all like to tell of our victories in life but most of us don't want to be perceived as a braggart. By asking, "What was your best financial decision?" we make bragging appropriate and socially acceptable. You are drawing on a positive emotion when you have clients report on their best purchase or investment. Also, you may find some clients will even volunteer the worst investment decision they ever made as well. Hearing this helps you tune in to the lessons they have and have not learned.

The successes that clients speak about here are deeply rooted in their emotions. You greatly increase your chance of making the right emotional connection by first listening to their unique investment autobiographical accounts.

We found some advisors who were quite comfortable, after hearing their clients' historical ups and downs, in sharing their own experiences as well. A sincere rapport often developed when clients heard their advisor talking about a mistake he or she made in the past and the lessons learned from the experience. Like the old quote, "Never trust a person who hasn't fallen off his horse 50 times," people like to know they are dealing with an unpretentious individual who is as comfortable discussing personal failures as personal successes. It can comfort clients to know that their broker/advisor has put the most expensive and disastrous lessons behind him or her.

I talked to an advisor who mentioned that he had started training as an advisor because he wanted to learn to avoid some of the foolish investment decisions he had been talked into when he was younger. He told me about some strategies that sounded good on the surface but were counterproductive. Rather than being afraid of an advisor who had made such mistakes, I was encouraged. I figured he'd been through the school of hard knocks and wouldn't be vulnerable to fads and foolish risks.

LESTER T., 70-YEAR-OLD CLIENT

Question #4: "Is There Anyone besides Yourself Whose Future Hinges on Your Financial Decisions?

This is an appropriate question for the baby boomer generation, many of whom now must face the prospect of supporting parents in their winter years who are not well provided for. Many boomers have thought fleetingly about what their responsibilities might be but have not come to the point of factoring those responsibilities into their own retirement plan.

A hundred years ago the average life expectancy was 44 and less than 4 percent of the nation's population was 65 or older. Today, a nonsmoking woman of 65 can expect to reach 87 and a nonsmoking man can expect to reach 85. The percentage of Americans over age 65 today is 20 percent and rising.

A hundred years ago the average life expectancy was 44 and less than 4 percent of the nation's population was 65 or older. Today, a nonsmoking woman of 65 can expect to reach 87 and a nonsmoking man can expect to reach 85. The percentage of Americans over age 65 today is 20 percent and rising.

Today's baby boomers face an expanding responsibility for the physical and fiscal well-being of their parents. Some boomers are deciding that they want to help their parents receive the care they need at home. Some must place their parents in a retirement home. Others are finding it more appropriate to take their parents into their own home. All of these decisions will involve financial planning on the part of the children involved if parents don't have substantial financial resources at their disposal.

Many of your clients may have faced these prospects clearly and realistically and have begun to factor in a percentage of their retirement portfolio toward parental care. If such a parental care scenario is remotely possible and you and your client have not sufficiently explored and planned for it, your client's retirement plan is not realistic.

My sister and I had periodically discussed how our parents were going to live in their retirement years but had never come to the point of analyzing what preparations we should make. Our mother had been a homemaker most of her life and most of our father's career was spent with a company that changed hands many times so that he ended up with a pittance for a pension. Our parents split after many years of marriage, which made their future financial prospects bleaker than ever. They both continue to work more than they wish to in what should be their retirement years.

My sister and I had felt a growing burden concerning their future over the years but never did anything but talk about it. An advisor introduced the idea to me and helped me to calculate how much I would need to contribute toward my parents' future. This advisor helped me to determine exactly what I needed to do for the next 10 to 15 years to fulfill this anticipated obligation. Even though my savings burden was increased, the emotional burden was lifted and I feel a thousand pounds lighter.

WALTER M., CLIENT

Walter's story points out a bitter irony in the 65+ population. In Chapter 10 we present a chart revealing that the average net worth of the 65+ client is $485,000. The key word here is *client*. Millions of individuals are not clients because they only have enough to just get by. One-third of all retirees reenter the job market within two years—some because they want to—but others because they have to. Forty percent of our older population lives in, or close to, poverty. Inflation and the loss of pension benefits through the death of a spouse loom as threats to retirees. At 5 percent inflation, today's maximum Social Security check will have 40 percent of its purchasing power, and in 20 years many of the people receiving these checks can expect to be around in 20 years. We must also factor in rising health care and drug costs and the toll they take on retiree income.

This group of retirees is not coming to you for advice because they have nothing to invest. It is their children who will come to you. Many of these baby boomers will see their cupidity interrupted and displaced by a moral obligation to help their parent(s) live a more noble lifestyle in their later years.

Question #5: Are There Any Stocks or Companies That You Would Not Care to Invest In as a Matter of Principle or for Moral Reasons?

We routinely ask audiences of brokers/advisors how many of them ask this sort of question. Only 5 to 10 percent of the brokers/advisors say that they do. When we asked clients this question, three out of five said they *did* have aversions to certain holdings based on personal scruples. Many people have strong aversions to investing in selected sectors, companies or even specific mutual fund companies in which they may have had a negative experience. Moral objections can range from mild to vehement, and any wise advisor will ascertain these objections in order to steer clear of them.

Socially responsible investing (SRI) is estimated by *Green Money Journal* to be a trend affecting close to $1 trillion, or a total of 10 percent of all invested assets. The morale issues driving the SRI trend range from environmental activism to indignation with tobacco.

Industry workshops with titles like "Integrating Money and Values" are becoming more common. SRI is about doing well—while doing good. People want to prosper but many people don't want to prosper in products, industries, or countries that they see as destructive. Growing numbers of investors are not interested in earning gains in countries that blatantly exploit human rights. Likewise, state lawsuits against tobacco firms and revelations of firms' child-focused marketing schemes stirred many an American's righteous feathers to the point of avoiding investments in those firms. Many mutual funds have begun to advertise the fact that they do not invest in tobacco. Pioneer Fund, for example, hasn't invested in tobacco since 1929 but didn't start marketing that fact until just recently.

Steve Scheuth, president of the Social Investment Forum (SIF), says research by his industry group has found close to 900 professionals who say they manage money in a socially responsible way. Scheuth said, "Quite a number of funds and a chunk of new dollars appeared out of nowhere because of this new awareness. People started talking about it."

Investors are beginning to hear that funds approaching investments with SRI are prospering. One example: Domini Social Equity Fund was named by the *Wall Street Journal* as one of the 65 best mutual funds with three-year annualized returns of 32.6 percent. Moral intangibles can be good for business—and they can be good for your business as well.

Consider some of these responses advisors have heard when asking this question about investing principles:

- A widow who lost her smoker husband to lung cancer
- The farmer's widow who blamed her husband's cancer on farm chemicals
- A man who blamed an HMO for his child's death
- People who have lost loved ones in crashes because of faulty transportation products or pilot errors
- Individuals who saw their communities polluted by certain industries
- Many individuals who have been downsized

There are also less tragic but nonetheless offensive experiences many clients articulated, such as these:

- The man who was repeatedly treated rudely by a certain national franchise
- The woman who suffered food poisoning at a national fast-food restaurant
- The woman who was treated unethically by a financial representative who sold her a certain mutual fund (The fund was a good performer but the association in her mind was so strong and distasteful that she preferred to invest elsewhere.)

The questions we use in the LIFE Discovery Model are intended to

- get your client talking;
- give you a depth of understanding with your client;
- stir emotions, values, and hopes; and
- help your client feel comfortable with your motives.

Values should be discovered before features are disclosed—otherwise, you end up with a bullseye on the wrong target! People would rather talk about their experiences than listen to your opinions.

The discovery paradigms that many advisors use are designed to gather facts, numbers, and, to a degree, investing experience. These methods of discovery do an infinitesimal amount of good toward building trust. In fact, what many such analytical questions may do is inspire the opposite—distrust—by giving the appearance that all you are interested in is your client's assets.

Remember:

- Values should be discovered before features are disclosed—otherwise, you end up with a bullseye on the wrong target!
- People would rather talk about their experiences than listen to your opinions.

Don't ever underestimate the fact that you are in the professional minority if you spend more time listening than you do talking.

The rule for asking a good question: the question invites you to reflect, and it compels you to answer.

Additional Questions That Good Advisors Ask

What have been your sources for learning about investing and what principles do you follow with your money?

I went to see a broker about some investment ideas, and one of the first questions he asked me was, "What principles or values have you followed with your money?"

I had not expected to hear that sort of question. I expected to be asked about my investment goals but not my beliefs about investing. It gave me great respect for this broker. He listened intently to my answers and then tried to guide me to investment strategies that matched my philosophies about money and investing. I left feeling as though he had a good grasp of what I could and could not live with.

NANCY J., CLIENT

Individual values toward money and investing can vary greatly:

- There are those who don't believe you can save enough, and there are those who believe you can't have enough to spend.
- There are those who want to leave nothing to their heirs, and there are those who want to leave all they can to their heirs.
- There are those who want to merely protect what they have, and there are those who want to "roll the dice."
- There are those who want to retire as soon as possible, and there are those who plan on never retiring.

If indeed your client is asking for education, then you are thrust into the role of teacher. The first thing you need to know in this role is where your student is on the learning curve. Question #3 in the LIFE Discovery Model zeroes in on that answer.

We found one broker who would ask, "What lessons have you learned about investing?" His clients would talk about their parents and both the positive and negative lessons they had gleaned from their parents' financial management or lack of it.

Even though the average net worth of those investors 65 and older is $485,000, there are millions in this age group barely scraping by on Social Security benefits and meager pensions. Many are forced to work part-time or full-time in their twilight years in order to survive. Their children who walk into your office as clients have devoted considerable introspection to their parents' dilemma. Many of these clients have learned some valuable lessons and have made clear resolutions about their own financial futures.

It is of immeasurable benefit for you to be aware of the principles clients have followed up to this point. You can match products to their principles and/or correct any erroneous ideas they have followed.

I've seen older clients who believe that in the end you'll always get burned in stocks and I've met younger clients who believe the stock market only goes up. I want to know my clients' beliefs about investing so that if I see a disparity in their thinking, I can work toward balanced expectations.

MARILYN W., ADVISOR

We have found that this question about investing principles also helps to reveal clients' sources of learning—whether parents, relatives, friends, financial letters, magazines and books, television, radio, the Internet, or other sources. It is illuminating to discover where clients have gathered their information and formed their principles of investment.

With the rising popularity of financial do-it-yourself philosophies, some of which have become best-sellers, investor gullibility has never been riper for the picking by purveyors of "dynamic investment vehicles."

Many think, with the advent of unprecedented access to market and investment information, that they can make most investment decisions on their own. All they need, they are told, is to follow the guidelines in the latest *New York Times* best-seller or the latest investment fad introduced by a friend.

Too often your clients fail to heed the old axiom, "Don't believe everything you read." Certain books have reached best-selling status by describing risky options trading as a can't-miss opportunity for investors. These books made millions by passing off ideologies that have caused people to lose millions.

The tidal wave of investment "information" available has often confused many of your potential clients and heightens the opportunity for the wise advisor who can help these individuals differentiate fads from principles. People need to be reminded of basic investment principles periodically to prevent them from making the wrong decisions. Principles have an anchoring effect. If sound investment principles are properly impressed on your client, even though she may occasionally drift (out of greed) toward fascination with fads like viatica settlements, penny stocks, options, and the like, your client will revert back to the reality of those principles.

This question about learning sources and investing principles helps you to become teacher-coach. Just as Vince Lombardi opened every training camp with, "Men, this is a football," so you as a professional advisor must always attend to the basic principles of investing with your clients. Some advisors even post principles of sound investing in their offices or send a printed version home with their clients.

Your clients take emotional comfort in knowing that you, as their broker/advisor, base your judgment on time-tested principles. It never hurts to remind clients of some of the following basic rules of investing:

- The relationship of risk to reward
- The power of consistent accumulation and compounding wealth
- The need for diversity
- The need for patience and thinking for oneself
- The need for emotional detachment from the market's manic fluctuations

These and other principles are basic attitudinal and behavioral guidelines that keep us true when tempted with impulsive financial behavior. Wise advisors seem to never stop reminding clients of the need for such principles.

A wise one hears and increases understanding.

PROVERBS 1:5

Other examples we could share abound but space doesn't allow. The lesson to be learned here is that brokers and advisors heard these stories because they asked the question about investing principles. They were all the wiser for asking—they could avoid potential emotional landmines and provide a harmonious relationship between their clients' money and values.

Why are you looking to move your account? One area many advisors inquire into is clients' previous investment relationships. Retirement specialist Spencer Hunt reported excellent success and client insight with this question, "Why are you looking to move your retirement account?"

Hunt safely assumed that if his client had come to move a 401(k) account some mistake(s) had been made or his client would not be moving the account, and he didn't wish to repeat those mistakes.

If his client had trouble articulating the reason for leaving, however, Hunt would prod with, "Is it because the fees are too high, the participation too low, or the communication insufficient?"

With this follow-up question, his clients would target their area of agitation. Hunt would forthrightly inform clients, "It's important to know why you want to do this because I may not be able to help you improve your situation." Clients appreciated his candor.

Other brokers/advisors asked that same question another way, "Have you had any experience with brokers/advisors before coming here?" No matter how you word it, however, it is helpful for you to know what sort of broker baggage or advisor afflictions your client may be carrying.

What do you want out of this relationship or what do you expect from me as an advisor? A good question triggers the imagination. This question has been used by financial advising pioneer John Sestina with great success in his 33+ years of advising clients. He asks each prospective client, "If we were to work together and it's now 12 months later, looking back a year, what did I do for you?"

What a terrific question! Sestina reports that no matter what expectations the client spoke about in the previous hour, his or her truthful expectations was elicited with that question. Sestina's question is a great closer. What better way for clients to leave the meeting than with the feeling that this advisor knows what they expect and will do their best to deliver.

And after the sale? One astute advisor offered the following gem.

> Two days after our meeting I call my client to ask, "How do you feel about the decisions we made? Are you comfortable with them?" I'm more interested in clients' emotional afterthoughts than anything. If insecurity or uncertainty persists, I want to address it now.

A feeling of calm and security as well as understanding what it is they have done with their money is what keeps clients content. The above after-sale question can help to ensure those emotions prevail.

The driving theme of this book is to help the financial professional become more astute and persuasive at telling the financial story. However, *the master storyseller understands that no dynamic in a sales presentation can equal the impact of getting your clients to tell their story.*

Reverse the 60-second clock and watch your performance escalate! John Sestina trains his advisors to make a point of timing how much they talk versus how much the client talks. "If you talk more than your client," Sestina teaches them, "you lose."

If you can discipline your tongue to defer to your ears and if you can adopt the Socratic approach and lead with questions instead of pushing with answers, you will win your clients' trust.

Your clients must leave with a feeling that your greatest interest is to know them and their personal needs. Advisor Jim Stout tells of once interviewing a widow for over 45 minutes when she suddenly stopped and asked, "Don't you want to know how much money I have?" (She had $8 million.)

"My greatest concern," Jim responded, "is to understand where you are coming from and to do what is right for you."

Jim Stout is a widower who knows that a big part of his job with those who have lost a mate is to help them through this troubled time in their life. "Trust," he says, "comes at the end of the relationship, not at the beginning."

6 | How Self-Deprecation and Wit Will Get You Further Than Self-Promotion

I not only use all the brains I have but all that I can borrow.

WOODROW WILSON

"My Lord," a certain nobleman is said to have observed after sitting next to Richard Bentley at dinner, "that chaplain of yours is a very extraordinary man." His Lordship agreed, adding, "Had he but the gift of humility, he would be the most extraordinary man in Europe."

OXFORD BOOK OF QUOTATIONS

Humor and humility. These are two basic competencies for the successful story-seller. When we asked clients about personal traits they most disliked in an advisor, the ones they often cited were overintensity and arrogance (another frequent complaint is confusing and boring presentations, which is dealt with in Chapter 2). Overintensity or overseriousness is often rooted in the personality traits of those who lack a sense of humor and/or who focus so much on results that relational aspects are disregarded.

From the clients' point of view, advisors who are overly serious in their approach are either stuffed shirts or anal retentive—or both! Advisors should work toward cultivating both humor and humility in their business relationships. In this chapter we discuss

- the role a self-deprecating approach can play in relieving tension in a client-broker relationship;

- how to help your clients get over the jargon jitters and start understanding what they are buying; and
- what role humor and humility play in top-producing personalities.

Humor is truth in intoxicated form.

The best sense of humor belongs to those who can laugh at themselves. We once met a salesman who was given a territory that had been devastated by previous representatives and opportunistic competitors; there had been five representatives in four years, and this territory was last in the nation for production. His sales manager told him if he could survive the first six months he would make it and warned him not to expect any warm fuzzy greetings by any potential clients. The sales manager's ominous warning proved to be an understatement.

The first businessman he visited was crass and egotistical. The man stood up and said, "Just turn around and walk right out. I have no interest in talking to your company or you. If you're smart, you won't come back."

This green salesman quietly turned to leave, stopped and said, "Sir, it will be hard to stay away—this is the warmest reception I've had yet." The businessman stared him down while trying not to laugh, but the dam broke and he laughed heartily at the resilient response.

"I can believe it," he said, "what's your name, kid? Give me your business card." The business owner warmed up and gave the salesman a short history of dealing with his company and previous representatives.

This salesman had to wait over two years to eventually procure that man's business, but the door may never have opened without self-deprecation and a ready wit. Humor is like a needle and thread—use it deftly and you can patch anything. Humor is also the lubricating oil of business that prevents friction and wins good will.

Have you ever noticed about those folks who take themselves so seriously . . . that no one else does?

MITCH ANTHONY

The first and greatest advantage of a keen wit and a self-deprecating approach is that it helps to relax the client. A relaxed client is a receptive client; a tense client is in a defensive state. Humor is unmatched in its ability to topple defenses.

In viewing client-advisor meetings, one can't help but notice the ebb and flow of comfort levels and the role the advisor plays in setting those levels. Your demeanor is like a thermostat setting the temperature for the meeting. When you are easygoing and cheery, laugh easily, and smile often, your demeanor is like a warm tropical breeze and your client relaxes. On the other hand, when you are grim, overly intent, and somber, your client grows tense.

SET THE EMOTIONAL TONE

True professionals have learned to accept responsibility for setting the tone for their meetings. You are responsible for controlling your own moods by exuding positive emotions and squelching negative ones. This can be accomplished by using self-deprecating humor and avoiding becoming defensive.

Daniel Goleman, in his brilliant book *Working with Emotional Intelligence*, wrote:

The transmission of mood is remarkably powerful. When three strangers, all volunteers for a study of mood, sat quietly in a circle for two minutes, the most emotionally expressive person transmitted his or her mood to the two others over the course of the two minutes. In every such session, the mood the most expressive person had going in was also the mood the other two felt coming out— whether happy, bored, anxious, or angry.

Emotions are contagious. Goleman maintains that evidence demonstrates we carry "emotional viruses" and spread them to everyone we meet.

You are responsible for controlling your own moods by exuding positive emotions and squelching negative ones. This can be accomplished by using self-deprecating humor and avoiding becoming defensive.

The emotional tone we want to set is one that is easygoing, relaxed, and even fun. Humor and self-deprecation prepare this environment in an almost magical way. Laughter and tension cannot exist in the same place at the same time. If you were carrying a heavy item and started laughing, you would probably drop the item or stumble. Why? The tension in your body is immediately released as laughter takes over! The ultimate presentation environment is one that is tension free.

A sense of humor can help you overlook the unattractive, tolerate the unpleasant, cope with the unexpected, and smile through the unbearable.

ANONYMOUS

I once visited a lawyer who won me over with his rare self-deprecating and down-home manner. He said to me as an introduction, "Feel free to interrupt me if I slip and use one of those million-dollar lawyer words that even Daniel Webster didn't understand. I'm just trying to get my money's worth out of law school. Excuse my desk if it looks a bit cluttered. I don't want you to think your case is going to get buried in that pile. I've got a dynamite assistant who tells me where to go and what to do. And I'm probably not the smartest lawyer who ever lived, but I've got a good sense of right and wrong and I fight like a bulldog."

I'd never met a professional so utterly devoid of self-importance, and I knew instantly that a person so realistic about his own strengths and weaknesses was worthy of my trust.

NATHAN T., CLIENT

A financial services client put it this way, "I know it's my money and it's serious business, but for crying out loud, show me some teeth, show me some personality! I don't want to have to feel uncomfortable every time I talk to my advisor about my money.

Is it possible that in an effort to appear the analyst and serious advisor, many have failed to demonstrate the softer skills of empathy and relatedness? Judging from client comments, it's apparent that clients are drawn to an advisor more on the basis of people skills than technical skills. And high on the list of people skills are both a modest view of oneself and one's adaptability.

How exactly does an advisor demonstrate the highly regarded trait of self-deprecation? It starts with one's attitude and manifests itself in conversation and behavior. Make these mental notes:

- Avoid being defensive.
- Admit mistakes quickly.
- Don't pretend to know things you don't.
- Learn to laugh easily at your mistakes.
- Don't expect presentations to always go perfectly.
- Learn from your mistakes instead of making excuses for them.

Warren Buffett often amuses and impresses with his ready admissions of poor judgment and his self-deprecating manner. Buffett confesses to dozens of investment errors, including the purchase of Berkshire Hathaway, the New England textile mill that is his holding company's namesake. An humble, self-deprecating manner is illustrated in these Buffett quotes:

"I want to explain my mistakes. This means I only do things I completely understand."

"At one time I had been investing with my glands instead of my head."

When Buffett was asked about an investment mistake, he is said to have replied, "I was a younger man and didn't know what I was doing at the time" (he was 53).

We call this sort of personality feature "folksy," "homespun," "down-to-earth." Critics will call it simplistic, but we know this—it sells!

When clients encountered brokers/advisors with humility and humor, their comments were:

"She's a real person, I can talk to her."

"No airs at all. I felt like I could trust him."

"He talked in a way I could understand. I want to know what's going on with my money."

"I felt like we got a lot done but had a lot of fun at the same time. That's the way I like to do things."

The one true measure of humility and self-deprecating humor is the ability to laugh at yourself. Can you find humor in your shortcomings, mistakes, and idiosyncrasies? Are you in touch with your "inner idiot"?

Clients trust what they call "real people" with professional skills. However, when you trust your analytical skills and knowledge more than your people skills, that's the day you're in trouble with people.

We all make mistakes. We all judge erroneously at times. People expect that. It's a part of the human condition. When a person can't show a little humility and humor regarding their fallibility, they end up making excuses for it and putting on pretenses. Excuses and pretenses are ultimate trust destroyers.

Clients trust what they call "real people" with professional skills. However, when you trust your analytical skills and knowledge more than your people skills, that's the day you're in trouble with people.

A Little Laughter Goes a Long Way

Do you know some good humorous quotes about investments, stocks, and the like? Use them to lighten the air and to bring a touch of levity to a serious task. Remember, humor and wit are your most powerful tools for stripping away defenses and building rapport.

Consider these classic lines involving investments from American humorist Will Rogers:

Rogers said to study the markets carefully before buying a stock, then . . . "When the stock doubles, sell it."

"But what if the stock doesn't double?" Rogers was asked.

He replied, "If it doesn't double, don't buy it."

Regarding the ethics of those who sell investments, Rogers said, "I'd rather be the man who bought the Brooklyn Bridge than the man who sold it."

Imagination was given to man to compensate for what he is not, and a sense of humor to console him for what he is.

ANONYMOUS

A person with a sense of humor doesn't make jokes out of life—he merely recognizes the ones that are there.

ANONYMOUS

Well Spoken

After all, when you come right down to it, how many speak the same language even when they speak the same language?

RUSSELL HOBAN

Brokers can help their clients get over the jargon jitters.

I hear these ads selling vocabulary development programs that promise to help you develop a Harvard vocabulary. Well, I don't want a Harvard vocabulary—I'm not even sure I want an Ohio State vocabulary. I want to speak a language every one of my clients understands!

JOHN SESTINA, ADVISOR EMERITUS, FINANCIAL AUTHOR, AND COLUMNIST

What language are you speaking to your clients? If your speech is tainted with "brokerese," you'd better stop and start speaking English again. The use of jargon repels clients and limits your bottom line. People are fed up with being talked around, talked down to, and confused. If you're not willing to speak a language your clients understand, they'll find a broker or advisor who will.

John Sestina puts it this way, "We advisors speak our own language, investing terminology, acronyms, etc., but this habit is more than annoying—it's always destructive. It's destructive to the client-advisor relationship."

Sestina goes on to analyze the reason many professionals (e.g., doctors, lawyers, advisors, etc.) talk over clients' heads—either they are insecure and want to impress or they are purposely keeping clients in the dark to maintain control. Neither motive has an ameliorative effort on a broker-client relationship.

The use of jargon to impress is the professional equivalent to what "trash-talking" ball players do on the basketball court. Like the great ones, financial services professionals ought to let their "game" do the talking for them.

The professional who speaks over the head of the client is useless to the client. Jargon dissuades the trust of the client and creates a distance in the relationship. John Sestina puts it colorfully when he says, "If someone is impressing you so much that you don't understand, fire him!"

According to clients we've spoken with, many of them are firing their advisors. Some are writing them off before they are hired because of jargon jitters.

I left the advisor's office feeling stupid. I didn't understand what he was talking about and he talked down his nose to me, I said, "No thanks," went home, called my dad, and said, "You handle it."

SHELLY B., AGE 32

I wanted to scream, "Slow down, this stuff may be second nature to you but it's not to me." I felt like I was riding 100 m.p.h. and was supposed to memorize every road sign along the way.

EDDIE Y., AGE 41

Every time I stopped or interrupted I felt like I was derailing his presentation. He'd glance at his watch and fidget nervously while I asked questions. I was thinking, "My God, this is my money we're talking about here."

MARTHA B., AGE 65

I'm sure this broker thought he was impressing the dickens out of me. As soon as he put on that scholarly I-know-this-is-over-your-head tone, I emotionally checked out of the presentation.

TOM T., AGE 35

I don't even know if this advisor knew she was doing it, but she mentioned so many terms I didn't understand that I felt extreme pressure to do something that I really wasn't sure about.

BRIDGET J., AGE 44

In some cases the use of jargon is unwitting on the part of advisors. Possibly they are so accustomed to speaking the investment language and lingo that it takes a fully conscious effort to move back into everyday English. In other cases, the use of jargon is consciously or unconsciously calculated. *The jargon that is designed to give the broker or advisor an edge ends up putting the client on edge.*

Warren Buffett wrote this regarding confusing footnotes in annual reports:

It's not impossible to write [an accounting] footnote explaining deferred acquisition costs in life insurance or whatever you want to do. You can write it so you can understand it. If it's written so you can't understand it, I'm very suspicious. I won't invest in a company if I can't understand the footnote, because I know they don't want me to understand it.

Nebulous language arouses suspicion. When you use nebulous language it arouses suspicion about the broker/advisor, not the product being described. Remember, the simple industry terms you take for granted are cryptic to many clients.

One investment professional told about his 94-year-old mother who doesn't understand the word yield. *She simply gives him a blank look. But if he says, "Give me $100 and you'll get $107 back at the end of the year," she understands. It's best to avoid jargon—period!*

Help Me Feel Smart

People don't want to appear stupid. Therefore, they'll neglect to ask questions if they perceive they're expected to understand the topic at hand. This is a natural and prevalent human insecurity. An advisor is much safer stopping to define any industry terms and have the customer tell you they already understand than it is to breeze through these terms with the assumption of comprehension. Again, we see a task that calls on the advisor to act as teacher. In this scenario the illumination of the pupil is reciprocated with trust by the pupil.

I've been advising for 20 years and always tell myself to stay away from jargon and eight-syllable words, but I find myself occasionally falling back into them. It takes a real conscious effort for me. When my clients leave, I find myself remembering the moments when they had apprehension and confusion written on their faces and it was then that I wish I had done a better job of communicating.

ELAINE B., BROKER

Kay Shirley thinks that advisors are doing a better job at realizing that their clients really do want to know what is going on. But she still hears too many stories from clients coming to her who are totally in the dark about what is going on with their money. Often, their previous brokers left them in the dark.

Kay speaks of clients coming to her with $1 million portfolios where brokers are assessing a 1.25 percent management fee each year and are not even bothering to take the time to explain specifically how the client's money is being invested and how fees are assessed. When clients ask brokers about it, they often hear answers in a language they don't understand. A case like this underscores the frustration jargon can create but also the void of trust left when a broker or advisor fails to communicate effectively. That $1 million portfolio is now being managed by an advisor who understands the importance of communication skills.

The beauty of the storyselling approach is that it makes jargon virtually obsolete. For every efficient term or concept, the storyseller has an illustration, an analogy, or another intriguing description to simplify the issue. Chapters 12 and 13 provide some excellent illustrations, metaphors, and anecdotes that we've gathered from accomplished storysellers in the financial services sector.

THE POWER OF WIT

An insurance company once did a competency study of its top tier of performers compared with the rest of the sales staff. The competencies they looked for were natural personal competencies that were not trained skills (selling skills, time management, etc.). Managers were asked what personal characteristics these people possessed that were crucial to their success. Four key competencies differentiated the top-tier performers from second-tier performers. As you went further down the ladder of achievement within the company, the differentiation became glaringly obvious.

The four competencies that constituted the necessary critical mass for success in this company's sales division were:

- Competitive spirit: Top-tier performers competed with themselves. They loved to win and abhorred not realizing their potential. They studied their competition and exploited their weaknesses by developing strengths in those areas.
- Achievementality: This refers to a mind-set that always asks, "What's next?" Individuals with this mind-set spent little time patting themselves on the back for successes and were concerned more with achievement than with rewards (financial payoffs). They did the necessary things needed to achieve even if they didn't come naturally.
- Teachability: The top-tier performers had an insatiable appetite for and curiosity about learning. They took instruction well and were not defensive. As one VP put it, "The hardest thing to find is a competitive spirit who listens well."
- Wit: This means quick thinkers with an ability to think on their feet. It includes an ability to use humor to deflate tension and win friendship and rapport. People with wit are self-deprecating and have modest opinions of themselves even though all of the top-tier performers were high in self-confidence. All had what customers called a likable demeanor.

The irony that this company discovered was that although it knew the above competencies were crucial, it did very little to screen for them in its hiring program.

We have touched on the last two competencies for success in this chapter: teachability and wit. Successful brokers/advisors have an humble, teachable quality that might seem paradoxical to their high self-confidence but isn't. It is actually the foundation of their confidence.

Self-deprecation, wit, humor, congeniality are also evident in top performers. They take life in stride, are in touch with their "inner idiot," and know that humor is simply truth in an intoxicated form.

7 | Making the Intuitive Leap with Your Client

The soul never thinks without a picture.

ARISTOTLE

Tom Rowley's job was to enroll the employees of various corporate clients into 401(k) plans that his firm provided. Tom soon learned that the barriers to his enrollment success were twofold—circumstantial and cerebral. He stated:

I would go into a place of business and try to sign people up over their lunch break, so time was working against me. The clientele were largely blue-collar workers with a very limited knowledge of investments. I was trying to enroll them into a program they didn't understand. Once they showed interest, they would become further confused by the allocation options they couldn't comprehend. I was supposed to accomplish all this in 10 to 15 minutes. The people seemed to stay away in droves.

Tom's dilemma was not unique. Clients steer clear of products that they struggle to understand even when they have an urgent need for the product. Their confusion repels the solutions they desire. It's like asking a hungry man to walk through a complicated maze to find a meal—he may find the confusion of the maze more off putting than the hunger pangs.

Tom Rowley had an intuitive flash and his natural storyselling ability kicked in. The remarkable response and results shocked him. Not only did he increase the number of enrollments but the amount of money allocated went up dramatically as well! Here's his story:

I was perplexed by this situation. You can't get people to buy into something they don't understand. It's like trying to help someone by making them feel stupid.

These people clearly were confused with the products I offered. I began to ask myself, "What illustration can I use to explain allocation options (aggressive growth, moderate risk, capital preservation, etc.) that is universally understood?" Then it struck me—everybody understands driving. All the corporate employees drive to and from work.

So I asked an employee, "Do you remember when the speed limit was 55? Well, let me ask you something, were you the kind of driver that drove 55 on the button, no faster? Or did you lock your cruise control onto 62 because you knew that in reality 62 was the limit? Or did you put statues of Jesus, Mary, and Joseph on the dash and put the pedal to the metal?"

The employee laughed out loud and immediately pointed out his driving habit— in this case 62 m.p.h. I made the correlation that he probably had a moderate risk tolerance and showed him the allocation option that best fit that level of tolerance. He signed up immediately and left with a smile on his face. I continued with this analogy and was amazed at how quick and efficient the process became. It was like we just leaped right past all the confusion and closed the deal. Not only did my enrollments rise but so did the dollar amount invested per employee.

Tom's 401(k) business skyrocketed when he discovered how to use *the intuitive leap.* The concept is simple: use concepts your client does understand to explain concepts he doesn't understand.

Once you discover the power of using metaphors to make intuitive leaps with your clients, you will abandon the crawl pace approach of statistic-laden presentations. Author Ned Herrmann put it this way: "A metaphor is a translation from one mental language to another, from the literal to the analogic. Its power is the instant understanding it brings by power of the translation."

An example of a metaphor is the "umbrella" of coverage that insurers sell to their clients. Just as nobody wants to be left in a rainstorm without an umbrella, no one wants to be exposed to life's unpredictable storms and disasters. Insurance companies provide a specific umbrella of coverage protecting their clients from the metaphorical downpour. This is an example of a metaphor that literally became a product, as every insurance contract uses language about "umbrellas" of coverage.

Instant understanding is brought to your presentation by applying appropriate metaphors. The payoff of instant understanding in your presentations is quicker and more confident client decisions.

As Tom Rowley discovered, application of a metaphor took his clients from thinking only to thinking and feeling. Suddenly his clients could relate as he used metaphors.

The purpose of communication is to get people to see and feel something. The majority of presentations used by brokers and advisors today don't accomplish those objectives. It is with the metaphor that we broaden the clients' understanding. Is it coincidental that the world's greatest communicators have been masters of the metaphor? It is futile to expect your client to learn a whole new set of principles and concepts. You teach the new by referring to the old and understood.

> The purpose of communication is to get people to see and feel something. The majority of presentations used by brokers and advisors today don't accomplish those objectives. It is with the metaphor that we broaden the clients' understanding. Is it coincidental that the world's greatest communicators have been masters of the metaphor?

Most people don't want or need to became fluent in investment industry jargon. However, most do want and need to became educated about the principles or concepts behind those confusing terms and prospectuses. As Tom found out, this need is especially apparent when selling retirement products.

Investment brochures and prospectuses are confusing to the average investor. Brochures and prospectuses for retirement products are in a class of their own with their confusing small print and voluminous information. Industry standards require massive amounts of disclosure resulting in thick, unreadable sales literature. Just the very sight of these materials is enough to scare people away. The stress, confusion, and mistrust aroused by small print only heighten the need for the broker/advisor to simplify and crystallize the principles and concepts of retirement investing. The storyseller achieves this objective with the clever application of persuasive illustrations and metaphors that enable the client to make the intuitive leap.

You advance or close the sale by stimulating the intuitive leap, thereby causing clients to feel the appropriate emotion. Whether it is excitement or fear, insecurity or peace of mind, the purpose is to sow the seeds of the emotion that will immediately stimulate their ability to decide.

DISCOVER YOUR CREATIVE POWERS

We have trained hundreds of brokers and advisors to become more adept at this art of metaphorical thinking with the instant analogy exercise. Here is how this exercise works:

Take a sales brochure for a specific product (a value-investing fund, an annuity, for example). Your job is to sell that product by using only an object in the room or on the table (e.g., clock, water glass, pen, candy, watch, chair). Test your presentations on other advisors for their feedback. This is a free association exercise that arouses an initial reaction of "paralysis by analysis"; it lasts about 30 to 60 seconds until you realize it's OK to think and talk outside Lipper or Morningstar.

The beauty of this exercise is that it helps brokers and advisors realize they have a creative thinking potential that they have not yet tapped. People are often amazed at the quick and creative associations their brain will make between the product and the seemingly unrelated object. We have often marveled at the simplicity and profundity of what participants come up with in the instant analogy exercise. The beauty of the approach is that you're translating something the client doesn't understand (the fund) into the language of an object they do understand.

Here is an example we heard from a broker who didn't consider himself a particularly creative individual. Holding a watch he began:

You know, it strikes me that a $10 watch and a $10,000 watch most of the time will tell you the same time. The uninformed or those easily fooled by appearances would have a hard time valuing those two watches and might overpay for the cheap watch or undervalue the expensive watch because it seemed to perform no better than the cheap watch. Observing this expensive watch, you can see that it has craftsmanship, components, and brand name value that the well-informed individual understands and appreciates. That is how our value fund operates. The fund's managers know what to look for to separate the superficial from the truly valuable. They know when people are paying too much for low-quality companies and not enough for high-quality companies.

Part of our problem is that we have been raised in schools that taught us there is one right answer for everything, and we therefore unconsciously buy into believing there is one right way for doing anything. When it comes to selling, there are a million right ways of doing things.

When this advisor shared his analogy with the group, he was met with warm applause. It was ironic to note the panic that was visible on the advisor's face when we first introduced the exercise.

You have a free-associative, metaphorical thought process that is waiting to be liberated. Part of our problem is that we have been raised in schools that taught us there is one right answer for everything, and we therefore unconsciously buy into believing there is one right way for doing anything. When it comes to selling, there are a million right ways of doing things. If it works, work with it. If it makes money, use it.

We watched hundreds of brokers/advisors come up with unique comparisons between an investment fund and a glass of water, just as we've seen scores of successful brokers and advisors use highly individualistic analogies to sell products and explain concepts.

We want you to be able to glean valuable and usable analogies and illustrations from this book, but a higher goal is to emancipate your own creative resources so you start thinking like a storyseller. We have seen individuals become so skilled and comfortable with this spontaneous form of communication that the only selling aid they use is a blank legal pad and a pen. You are limited only by your imagination.

One of the most humorous and daring examples of using an analogy to make a difficult sale came to us from Paul, an insurance broker . . .

I was trying to land the account of a large business owner who told me he didn't want to hear about coverages, features, and the like. He wanted the lowest price—period. Whoever gave him the lowest quote would get the account. I was amazed at his myopic approach. Since he had demonstrated such a poor understanding of why a person buys insurance, I decided I had nothing to lose, so I took a creative approach.

For our next appointment I prepared two proposals. Proposal #1 had no coverage and a premium of $1 a year. Proposal #2 had the needed coverages and the accompanying premium. On my way to his office I stopped and bought a plunger.

When I walked into his office he looked at me, the plunger in my hand, back at me, and asked, "What's that for?"

"Oh, I'll get to that shortly," I promised, "first, let's do our paperwork."

"O.K.," he laughed nervously and I sat down.

"Jim," I asked, "you told me that price was your one and only consideration, right?"

"Right."

I handed him proposal #1. "I'm confident that on the basis of price, this proposal will not be beat."

"OK, Paul, are you trying to be a smart aleck or what?" he said to me, showing some annoyance.

I grabbed the plunger and put it on his desk. "That brings me to this. It struck me on the way in here today what an unpleasant thing it is to have to buy insurance. You buy insurance hoping you never have to use it. It's an awful lot like this plunger that I stopped to buy on my way here. You don't buy a plunger hoping you'll get to use it. But should the need ever arise for one and you don't have one that works . . . well, you're going to find yourself knee deep in it and you're not going to be a happy man."

I had a silent, nervous moment as he stared at me, then the plunger, and surmised the situation. A slight grin broke out on the corner of his mouth, and he asked, "Do you have a real proposal?"

I handed him proposal #2, answered his questions, and to my surprise he told me he was giving me his account.

As I left, he shook my hand and said, "That was awfully bold coming in here like that, but you made your point."

Paul told us, "I knew this man well enough to know he wouldn't listen to any rationale I could offer about better coverage at a higher price. With this bit of drama, I figured he would think I was either nuts or brilliant, and I hoped he would respect me for telling the truth."

Although it is not necessary to display such panache and showmanship to be a successful storyseller, we think Paul's story illustrates the fact that an analogy can unlock decisions that a reasonable explanation won't touch. Reasonable explanations arouse defenses. Analogies arouse curiosity. When you learn to use the intuitive leap in your presentations, clients will have an easier time deciding. This translates into less time explaining for you, and ultimately more assets under management.

HOW TO MAKE MORE BY TALKING LESS

One good illustration can save you 60 minutes worth of explanation, reasoning, justification, comparison, and analysis. Top producers have come to the realization that clients must buy in emotionally to the concept before they will act. An incisive illustration is the most efficient route to this buy in. When you view the traditional, reasoning-centered approach to selling, you see immediate flaws, as illustrated in Figure 7.1.

The typical selling approach follows a linear path. For clarity sake, let's define A, B, C, D as:

A = Our product, which we perceive to be the **answer.**

B = Why we think others should **buy** our product.

FIGURE 7.1 Linear Sales Process

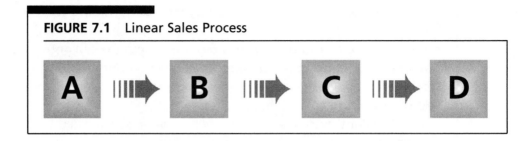

C = We add more **compelling** reasons to buy.
D = Get a **decision.**

We present a product (A) that we think or hope will answer clients' needs. We start telling them about features (B) such as ratings, rankings, performance, history, and so on. Traditionally, at this point we wait for objections and attempt to meet those objections with more compelling logic (C). Finally, hoping our powers of persuasion and reasoning have prevailed, we invite a decision (D).

A presentation process that relies exclusively on linear logic is inherently flawed. First, it fails because it fails to engage the clients' emotions or imagination. Lou Gerstner, CEO of IBM, once said, "You've got to appeal to people's emotions. They've got to buy in with their hearts and bellies, not just their minds." Second, reasoning-based presentations invite objections. Third, step-by-step logical explanations take up valuable time that could be spent listening to clients.

Another problem occurs when we try to get a decision. Clients raise their objections and we answer with more proof. Now their objections go underground and are unspoken. We are now trying to close over these unspoken objections. Maybe this is the reason why one out of three clients said they felt pressured to buy something they weren't sure about. Reason is overrated. As successful salespeople have discovered, about 80 percent is emotion and 20 percent logic. (See Figure 7.1, Linear Sales Process.)

When we tell you this product has four stars out of five and is ranked 29th out of 189 peer funds, we're inviting a comparative objection. For example, "Which one is ranked first and has five stars?" If my client doesn't say it, he or she is likely thinking it. Instead of overcoming objections, the intuitive leap moves right past them to the emotional or imaginative trigger that causes the decision to be made. What we have witnessed with top storysellers is the ability to tell a story or share an analogy or illustration that hits the emotional bullseye and then minimizes the need for explanation, justification, comparison, and reasoning.

The efficient sales method (assuming sufficient discovery) has been completed to share what the product is, give an illustration that helps clients feel comfortable and clear about how it works (A), and inquire whether the product fits their need (D). If, at this point, clients have questions about particular features and analysis, you can work backward to those areas (B). Why spend so much time explaining details that may not be necessary (C)? Once clients are emotionally secure and calm with the product or service, the issue is settled. They can take the prospectus home and study it if they wish. The best use of your time is for you to get to know the clients (See Figure 7.2, Intuitive Leap).

The illustrations, analogies, and metaphors shared in this chapter and later chapters are designed to help you meet the emotional as well as rational needs of your clients. If your clients don't have a good feel for the idea you're promoting, all the rationalization in the world won't alter that feeling. You'll save yourself time and frustration by using well-timed and clearly targeted illustrations and analogies to enlighten your clients.

Brokers and advisors who have mastered this skill have to spend far less time explaining details and overcoming objections. These individuals have discovered how to utilize the intuitive leap.

SELLING THE INTANGIBLE

Effectiveness in using the intuitive leap with your clients is contingent in part on your ability to empathize with their most pressing intangible needs. Brokers/advisors with a strong social radar (empathy) are best at picking up on what cli-

FIGURE 7.2 Intuitive Leap

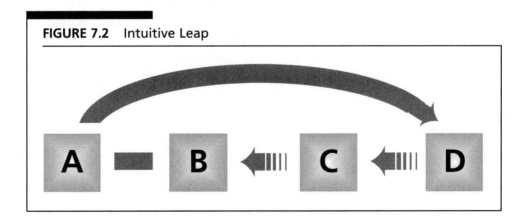

ents' intangible needs are. Clients don't come to you simply because they want to buy stocks, bonds, mutual funds, or annuities. Rather, clients come because they want hope, freedom, status, independence, security, peace of mind, stability, and simplicity in financial affairs—or any other number of intangible needs. These needs pulsate within the clients. They look to you to pick up on and address those needs.

You must develop your social radar to pick up these particular needs. This radar will be the most potent skill you can possess. This skill can only be developed by being a totally involved listener tuned in to the emotion of the client, not tuned in to the assets.

You must develop your social radar to pick up these particular needs. This radar will be the most potent skill you can possess. This skill can only be developed by being a totally involved listener tuned in to the emotion of the client, not tuned in to the assets.

Be able to sense what others feel without having them first tell you. Clients don't usually reveal their feelings in words; they tell us with their tone of voice, facial expressions, and body language. But they do tell us. People walk into your office with core hopes and fears. Your goal ought to be to pick up what those hopes and fears are and then meet or answer them.

We asked investors this question, "What need were you feeling inside that made you want to see an advisor or broker?" Here are some of the answers we heard:

- "I'm afraid I'm not doing the right things with my money."
- "I don't want to be burdened with details."
- "I'm afraid of ending up like my folks, old and scraping by."
- "I just want to simplify all these investments. It's too hard to keep track of them all."
- "I want to make sure my family is taken care of."
- "I want the freedom to do what I want with my life ten years from now."
- "I don't believe you can ever have enough."
- "I want to keep what I have and maintain my lifestyle."
- "I need to talk to someone who knows what he's talking about."

FUD

There is a palpable sense of fear, uncertainty and doubt (FUD) within every client. Clients may say they have hopes but what they really have is a fear that their hopes won't be realized. The intuitive, empathetic advisor has learned to pick up on this intangible fear, uncertainty, and doubt with their social radar and can work toward allaying that fear. Investors are motivated by two things: (1) something to be gained (greed); and (2) something to be lost (fear).

Studies show that fear of consequences is by far the greater motivator (3:1 ratio). You can and should talk about goals and the future. The fact is, however, that many people have trouble visualizing a future goal and don't possess the discipline to stay on course. They, have no trouble, however, visualizing the past and know for a fact that they do not want to go backward! We suggest focusing on a product or service that answers their most potent fear. All people fear something regarding money. Many fear not getting enough; others fear not keeping what they've gathered.

A guy who came to me told me he had big plans to retire at 45 and see the world; he was all optimism and smiles. He was 37 years old and had made a lot of money and had spent a lot of money. I began to see a pattern that this fellow, despite his many talents, lacked discipline. He never said it, but I sensed that he feared he would not be disciplined enough to reach his early retirement. I honed in on that and described a disciplined approach to retirement. I told him if he would allow me to design a plan and comply with it, he would reach his goal. He left my office calm and secure that I was going to help insulate him from his own impulsiveness, a quirk I've discovered in many clients.

GARY K., ADVISOR

In this case, it was the fear of impulsive behavior that brought the client to the advisor. Each of us is unique in the fears and uncertainties that we all have. We have witnessed successful brokers and advisors who have developed their social radar sufficiently to be able to decipher others' intangible emotional needs. Too many brokers and advisors are so intent on selling a particular product that they tune out or ignore the message of fear and uncertainty coming from a client. They aggressively push through their preparations and ignore all emotional cues. They are so intent on selling that they miss the sale.

Your job regarding an intangible need is simple: find it and meet it. Empathy is not just hearing what the client tells you. Empathy is the ability to read between the lines. In selling products, you are actually selling emotions—the essence of intangible selling. Tangible success comes to those who can read their clients' intangible needs.

IRRESISTIBLE EMOTION

The logic of helping clients "feel" something is the reason why a car salesman has potential buyers get in and drive the car they are interested in. The salesman wants them to feel the comfort, sniff that alluring new car smell, and feel the acceleration and the grip of the tires as they go around the curve. Once potential buyers put their hands on that wheel and have that multisensory experience, they are well on their way to rationalizing their need to own this particular vehicle.

How does that car-driving experience compare with looking at a brochure? It's not even close. There is a very limited imaginative and emotional appeal with literature. We need to help our clients *feel* something.

TRY IT ON

We have found that the best salespeople in every realm literally get their clients to "try on" their product. This of course is much easier to do with high-ticket tangible items like cars and expensive watches, but this same skill is utilized every day by skilled storysellers to sell intangible products like investments. Let yourself feel the difference between saying, "This investment will yield 6 percent" and "This investment will make a check payable to you every month for $284. How does that sound?" Now, that is letting your client try on the investment. By going from a sterile mathematical transaction to visualizing the bills that they will pay with that income, we have brought our presentation to the feeling level.

Our brains work in an irresistible, automatic patterning system. When we hear a word such as *wedding*, neurological connections automatically kick in to our memory banks, and certain pictures and emotions are instantaneously evoked. The same pattern takes place when we hear any word related to our life experience. It could be a color, a name, a place, a goal, or a job that is mentioned, and our brain will retrieve the pictures and emotions first and the information later.

Whenever I see a blue one-and-a-half-story house, I am taken back to the house I lived in when the kids were young, and I'm instantly hit with a flood of emotions and a collage of images. We are visual and emotional creatures as well as rational creatures. All storyselling does is to recognize this fact and play it into the selling process.

The intuitive leap with illustrations, analogies, and metaphors is simply playing to the visual side of clients' brains. Once they "see" it, they understand it. Facts, statistics, and claims are difficult to "see."

The intuitive leap with illustrations, analogies, and metaphors is simply playing to the visual side of clients' brains. Once they "see" it, they understand it. Facts, statistics, and claims are difficult to "see."

When you bring up words like *retirement, goals,* and *hopes,* tune in not just to what the clients say but to the emotion in their words. Get a picture of what they are describing and demonstrate to them that you can see that picture and the path necessary to arrive at their goals.

Making the intuitive leap with your clients saves time and results. You'll see more assets invested because the leap gives clients an image to focus on. It also satisfies the emotional need that must be met to make an investment decision. There is a reason successful brokers and advisors present this way—their business grows in leaps when they use the intuitive leap. Or as Tom, the 401(k) specialist, put it, "Once the 'light comes on,' the pocketbook gets opened."

8 | Using Analogies and Metaphors to Move Your Clients and Products

The greatest thing by far is to be the master of the metaphor.

ARISTOTLE

Every broker or advisor who has depended on a commission to pay the rent knows how indispensable closing skills are to sales success. Competent discovery and dynamic presentation are wasted if a deal is not struck. One former retirement advisor put it this way:

I had great people skills. People liked me. I could get them to talk. My product presentations were passionate and entertaining, but I just couldn't pull the trigger and get the sale closed. I was afraid of what the client might feel if I was advancing too quickly. I went broke in six months and went back to teaching.

As Tom Rowley discovered, with the right analogy, clients make an intuitive leap toward closing the sale. The analogy of driving at 55 m.p.h. stirred the emotion needed to unlock the volitional process. Simply put—stir the right emotion and decisions are easy!

The reason so many people find closing to be difficult is because they sense that the proper emotions that must be triggered before they can make a decision have not yet been triggered. Closing is awkward when we offer statistics and information that are emotionally irrelevant to a client and then press that client for a decision while he's in an apathetic, confused, or hostile state. The very fact that the seller attempts to close a sale while a client is in this state reveals an utter lack of empathy for the client's emotional state. From the client's point of view, the awkward close also reveals the true motivation of the seller. Clients tacitly assume that self-interest is the broker's guiding force if they fail to tune in to resistant or uncertain emotions. The storyseller resolves those emotional quandaries before advancing or closing the sale.

In this chapter we describe how to use the intuitive leap to increase your business. We will look at the following:

- The tools of persuasion used in the intuitive leap (illustrations, analogies, metaphors)
- How stimulating intuitive leaps will increase your performance and income, shorten the sales cycle, make objections obsolete, and garner larger investments
- How to read and meet the client's intangible need (People buy to meet or placate internal, intangible needs; the most successful brokers and advisors know how to read between the lines and sell to the intangible need.)

TOOLS OF PERSUASION

il′lus•tra′tion: an example or instance that helps make something clear
a•nal•o•gy: a resemblance in some particulars between things otherwise unlike; similarity
met•a•phor: a figure of speech in which one thing is spoken of as if it were another

THE ILLUSTRATION

The use of illustrations can add dynamic impact to your sales presentations. A simple illustration draws the eyes and attention of the client. For those with less than genius artistic ability, stick drawings will do! When used in savvy fashion, illustrations can act as riddles that the broker or advisor will solve. In fact, sometimes an illustrated riddle is just what the advisor ordered.

Outstanding storyseller Kay Shirley uses the following illustration when confronted with clients who have difficulty comprehending the importance of diversification. She draws two boxes on a piece of paper (see Figure 8.1) and then asks the client, "What are these?" They might respond, "A birthday cake"; however, most will simply answer, "I don't know." Kay responds, "These are elevators. Now, let me ask you that were there an earthquake, which one would you rather be on?"

FIGURE 8.1   Kay Shirley's Illustration of Diversification

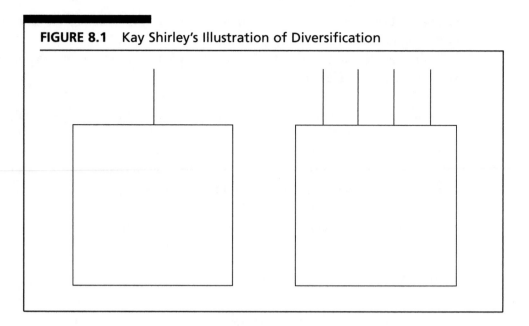

With a simple illustration, Kay is able to explain *and convince* her clients in a way most people can't accomplish with an hour of reasoning. This is an example of an intuitive leap. Use this illustration and observe your clients' response. You may see, as we have, that your clients may nod, laugh, smirk, or say things like, "I like that" or "I get it now" or "That's good—very good."

Kay's illustration uses a number of storyselling elements as described below:

- She illustrates the concept.
- She uses an analogy most people can relate to.
- She asks an intuitive question (most individuals do not have to think long to know which elevator they'd prefer in a crisis).
- She persuades the client with emotion (safety).

Building a House

When explaining the role the financial advisor plays, Paul Basabelle likes to draw a picture of a house. He says a simple stick drawing will do (see Figure 8.2). Paul says to his client:

FIGURE 8.2 Paul Basabelle's Stick House

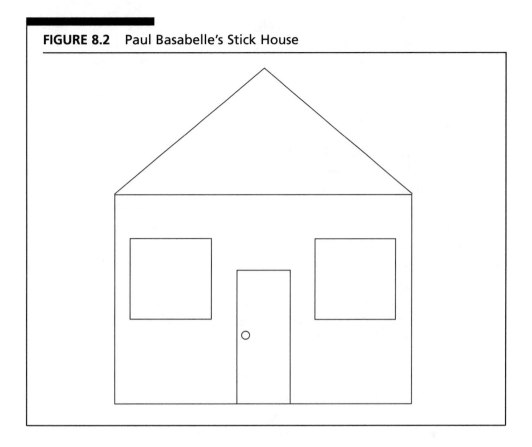

I don't know what your dream house looks like (I hope nothing like this). Maybe you've already built it or maybe you're going to build it someday. I draw this because in creating a financial plan, truly you are the architects of your home. You know what you want to live in someday. You've got a picture in your mind. My role is that of the general contractor you would hire to make sure the best skilled laborers are hired to build your house. If there are tax issues we'll need an accountant; if there's a will or trust, we'll need an attorney. Possibly equities, bonds, and annuities will be a part of this dream home. My role is to find the best people or companies for all those features and bring them altogether to build your dream house. To do that job well, I've got to get a good picture of what your dream house looks like. What kind of rooms, fixtures, windows, and features does it have?

And with that Paul begins his discovery process of ascertaining his client's hopes, goals, and realities. Paul says people always seem to warm to this illustration. Most people have thought of building a dream home and find the topic easier to relate to than drafting a financial plan.

The Confidence Meter

Sandra, a retirement specialist, shares what she calls the confidence meter with her clients. She draws a horizontal line beginning with zero and ending with 10 and 5 in the middle (see Figure 8.3).

Sandra then asks her client, "Mr./Mrs. Jones, this is what I call my retirement confidence meter. With zero being the least and 10 being the most, how confident are you right now that you'll be able to retire when you want with as much as you'll need?" She hands the pen to her clients and they place a mark somewhere on the line.

Clients will often indicate a relatively low number. Toward the end of the session, Sandra pulls out the original confidence meter and says, "I want to go back to our retirement confidence meter with the same question. Based on the ideas we've discussed, how confident are you feeling that you will be able to retire when you want with as much as you'll need?"

Some will mark a slight improvement and others will mark a major improvement. Any improvement is progress. The clients now have a visual, subjective expression in front of them that will help them actually feel the progress they are making.

Sandra tells her clients that her goal is to get them to a 10 so that they can live without the stress of wondering if and when they will make it to retirement. She

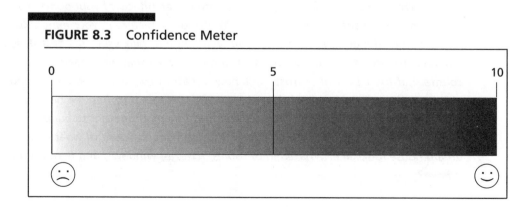

FIGURE 8.3 Confidence Meter

0   5   10

assures her clients that although it may take some time to get there, she will work with them until they arrive—and afterward, to stay on track.

The storyseller works to trigger appropriate emotions necessary for making decisions. This confidence meter reminds the clients why they came to a retirement specialist in the first place. We'll feature more stories in Chapter 13.

A TIME-TESTED METAPHOR

One time-tested, highly effective metaphor that brokers and advisors use to successfully explain both market volatility and/or value investing principles is Benjamin Graham's Mr. Market.

I'd like to tell clients that if we want to be successful we should find the most successful investor we can and do what he or she does. It would be hard to find an example better known or more successful than Warren Buffett. People recognize the name. I tell my clients that I've studied Buffet and found that he credits much of his success to two people. The first was his college professor and mentor Benjamin Graham, who taught Buffett the "10 Rules of Value Investing" and the second person was someone introduced to Buffett by Graham, Mr. Market.

Mr. Market is the perfect metaphor for the schizophrenic and illogical behavior of the markets in general and of stocks in particular. It seems to calm people about constant fluctuations and encourages them to stay above the manic mind-set.

KYLE D., BROKER

Ben Graham taught Warren Buffett to watch Mr. Market very closely and to profit from his mistakes. Here is what Ben Graham wrote about Mr. Market:

You should imagine stock quotes as coming from a remarkably accommodating fellow named Mr. Market, who is your partner in a private business. Without fail, Mr. Market appears daily and names a price at which he will either buy your stock or sell you his.

Even though the business that the two of you own may have economic characteristics that are stable, Mr. Market's quotations will be anything but. For, sad to say, the poor fellow has incurable emotional problems.

But like Cinderella at the ball, you must heed one warning or everything will turn into pumpkins and mice: Mr. Market is there to serve you, not to guide you. It is his pocketbook, not his wisdom, that you will find useful. If he shows up someday in a particularly foolish mood, you are free to either ignore him or to take advantage of him, but it will be disastrous if you fall under his influence.

At times he waxes euphoric and can see only the favorable factors affecting the business. When in that mood, he names a very high price because he fears that you will snap up his interest and rob him of imminent gains.

At other times he is depressed and can see nothing but trouble ahead for both the business and the world. On these occasions he will name a very low price, since he is terrified that you will unload your interest on him. Under these conditions, the more manic-depressive his behavior, the better for you.

One other fella we might mention here is Mr. Market's best friend, Mr. Media. Mr. Media loves to take his cues from Mr. Market and shout them in the streets and over the airwaves.

One day it is, "The market is up 100 points—buy everything!" The very next day Mr. Media shouts, "The market is down 100 points—run for the hills!"

A recent article in USA Today reported exactly the situation we just described. The headline reads, "When market falls, media stoke investors' fears."

An effective metaphor like Mr. Market helps the client make a necessary intuitive leap when buying an equity or equity-related product—seeing market volatility as their ally, not their enemy!

Every client can relate to dealing with foolish and manic personalities. The Mr. Market metaphor, like all good metaphors, helps clients see matters in a brand-new light. The very factors that once kept clients awake with stress may now keep them awake with anticipation. Foolish investor behavior is an emotional issue, not an intellectual issue. Metaphors speak to the emotional side of the brain. A good metaphor brings an image, a picture to a previously disturbing emotion and literally transforms that emotion. Maybe that is what Aristotle meant when he said the soul never thinks without a picture.

If you think of a metaphor or analogy and wonder if it will work its magic, there's no proving ground like a presentation. Before you put your idea on stage, however, you may want to put it through our metaphor grid.

> **E**very client can relate to dealing with foolish and manic personalities. The Mr. Market metaphor, like all good metaphors, helps clients see matters in a brand-new light. The very factors that once kept clients awake with stress may now keep them awake with anticipation.

Metaphor Grid

1. **Is it a natural or common analogy that anyone can relate to?** Analogies from nature are more effective than technical analogies—for example, "It's kind of like a tree" versus "It's kind of like a computer."

I think the fact that I grew up on a farm has helped me as an advisor. I've been able to relate a lot of investment ideas to the laws of nature I learned as a farmer. Also, being a farmer gave me a profound understanding of risk and volatility.

PAUL B., ADVISOR

Harvard University once did a study on mental agility with metaphorical thinking and found that those raised close to nature had greater mental dexterity with metaphorical thought. It also found that metaphors from nature were more vivid and provocative than those from urban settings. Example: Subjects were asked to complete this sentence, "He was as slow as . . .". A subject with an urban background wrote, "As slow as an old car hitting on one cylinder." A subject with a rural background wrote, "As slow as a pregnant cow with diarrhea." *Lesson:* Lean toward natural analogies whenever possible.

2. **Does it bring light or temporary puzzlement?** A good analogy should be neither too obvious nor too baffling.

3. **Does it trigger the target emotion?** Find metaphors and analogies that communicate your target emotion; patience, safety, balance, growth, or the like.

4. **Does it bring the "Aha" response?** Metaphors are most effective when they bring new perspectives to old ways of viewing things. A good metaphor can open up instantaneous understanding and comprehension. Try it out with clients. Does it evoke positive comments and affirmative body language?

The soul never thinks without a picture. That is why smart advisors use "picture" words. These "picture" words arouse the kind of feelings that are guaranteed to move your clients and your products.

PART THREE

Storyselling in Desirable Markets

9 | Telling the Story of the Affluent

So far in this book we have explained *how* the best advisors operate. These successful advisors have learned to truly listen to and understand their clients and are skilled in telling the financial story with easy-to-understand metaphors and stories. Now, we will show *where* top advisors are practicing these skills. In this section we highlight the three top sectors of society where burgeoning wealth is to be found: the Affluent market (investable assets of $250,000 or greater), the Mature market (those over 60) and the Women's market.

Although these fast-growing markets are obvious to the astute advisor, they are not always easy to penetrate or prosper in. We believe that you, by taking a story-seller's approach to these markets, can positively differentiate yourself from all the other advisors they have heard. Any financial advisor can quote returns and recommend asset allocation, but it takes an exceptional advisor to really listen to clients' stories, connect with their core personality, and describe financial matters in a language they understand. This and the following chapters on the Mature and Women's markets will give you an emotional blueprint to work with to better connect with each of these prospering groups.

There are some things that money will change—and some things that money will not change. Having money doesn't change the core emotional make-up and personality of a person. Just because some of your clients have acquired $600,000 or $6,000,000 in investable assets does not mean the essence of who they are will be changed. These wealthy clients are people—people with unique stories to tell and emotional concerns to connect with. These clients are guided in their purchase decisions by a "gut feeling" like any individual on any tier of wealth. It is important to remember that the right side of the wealthy person's brain works the same as that of any other person when it comes to buying decisions. By studying these three chapters you will gain invaluable insight on how to forge a relational connection with the growing affluent classes of our society.

PURSUING THE AFFLUENT INVESTOR

The increasingly competitive pursuit of the affluent investor has created new challenges for investment representatives. Not only is it harder to win new clients but also to retain existing ones. The affluent investor is defined as someone who has $250,000 or more in investable assets. Research shows affluent investors will reward their investment representative with their loyalty so long as the relationship is managed in a high-quality way.

The amount of investable assets of the affluent market is staggering. In the United States, $23 trillion is in private hands, according to Prince & Associates. Half of that amount, or $11.5 trillion, is concentrated in the hands of affluent investors, just 4 percent of the population. (See Figure 9.1.) The question becomes, how can you more effectively sell, retain, and gain referrals from this market?

One answer is *The Nine Lives of the Affluent.* This program was developed by Van Kampen Funds from several sources, including Russ Alan Prince, a leading authority on affluent investors. It is based on nearly 900 in-depth interviews with affluent investors by Prince & Associates. *The Nine Lives of the Affluent* has empirically identified nine profiles, or psychological types, that allow you to better

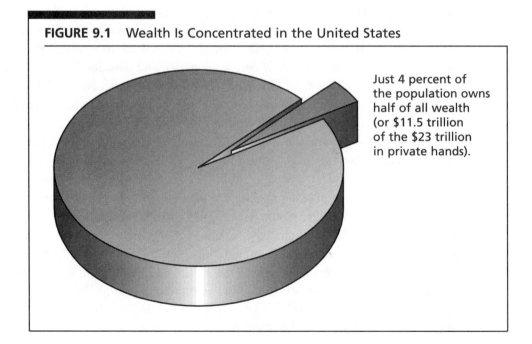

FIGURE 9.1 Wealth Is Concentrated in the United States

Just 4 percent of the population owns half of all wealth (or $11.5 trillion of the $23 trillion in private hands).

understand the motivations, concerns, and needs of the affluent investor. Each of the nine profiles will help you tailor your sales approach for greater client satisfaction, learn what products and services each type wants to know more about, and discover what traits each type looks for in an investment representative. Ultimately, if affluent clients perceive that you understand their investment style, they will entrust you with more assets and referrals of their affluent friends. Affluence does not change a person's need to be understood—if anything it amplifies that need.

It should come as no great surprise that clients judge you according to investment performance and service. However, what is surprising is the level of importance placed on these two areas. Research shows clients regard their relationship with advisors as four times more important than investment performance in their overall satisfaction. Investment performance alone will not carry the day. The good news is that investment representatives who can deliver solid investment performance combined with high-quality customer service are well positioned to increase the amount of assets on deposit per affluent client as well as win referrals from their existing clients.

HOW TO GET YOURSELF FIRED

Of all the affluent clients who fired their investment representative, 87 percent did so because of the relationship (13 percent because of investment performance). In fact, clients will leave even if investment performance is high.

Of all the affluent clients who fired their investment representative, 87 percent did so because of the relationship (13 percent because of investment performance). (See Figure 9.2.) In fact, clients will leave even if investment performance is high. Ninety-six percent of clients who fired their representative because of the relationship were "very happy" with the investment performance. However, if the relationship is strong, your business will be too. One in four highly satisfied affluent clients will increase assets under management each year. Better still, nine out of ten highly satisfied affluent clients will refer at least one person who becomes a client. The operative words here are *becomes a client,* not just a referral.

Perceptual Map Worksheet: How Affluent Investors Rate Financial Services Providers

It is important to understand both thought processes and perceptions when dealing with the affluent—what they think and what they think of you. The perceptual map

FIGURE 9.2 Why Clients Leave

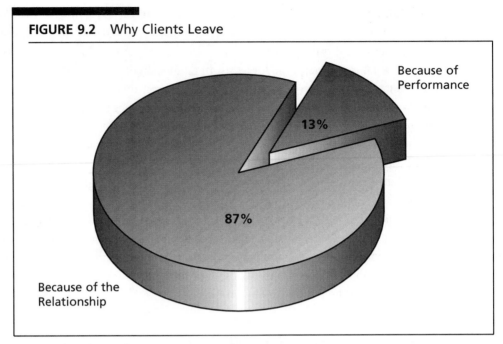

Source: Prince & Associates

(see Figure 9.3) helps you with the latter. It not only tells you how you are perceived by the affluent according to service quality and investment expertise but how your competition is perceived as well. Think of it as an industry road map. To reach the affluent, you first need to comprehend your present location in their perceptions.

How closely does your perception of the following nine financial services providers match the research? In Figure 9.3, simply plot the following financial services providers according to the level of service quality and investment expertise you believe they provide (10 being the highest ranking).

1. Mutual fund companies
2. Discount brokers
3. Independent money managers
4. Financial consultants
5. Full-service brokers

6. Family offices
7. Financial planners
8. Private banks
9. Insurance providers

(See Figure 9.3 "Perceptual Map Worksheet.")

FIGURE 9.3   Perceptual Map Worksheet

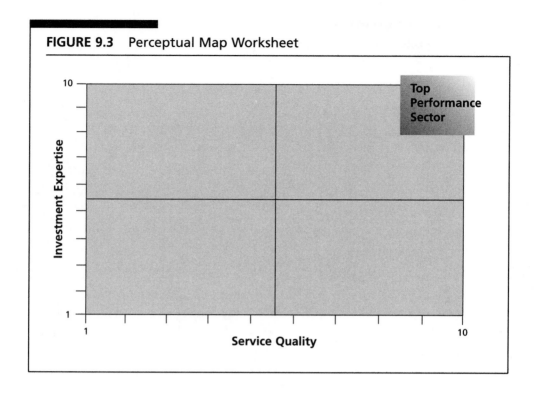

Russ Prince's 900 interviews with the affluent turned up these perceptions (see Figure 9.4):

- Full-service brokers were at about the middle of the pack on both investment expertise and service quality.
- Financial planners ranked slightly higher in both categories in affluent perceptions.
- Independent money managers received the highest marks in investment expertise and were second highest in service quality.

What is the most expeditious path to achieving greater status in perceptions of the affluent? It is to demonstrate to each affluent investor that you possess a clear understanding of each one's idiosyncratic investment motives and style. This is where *The Nine Lives of the Affluent* profiles can be of help.

FIGURE 9.4 Completed Perceptual Map

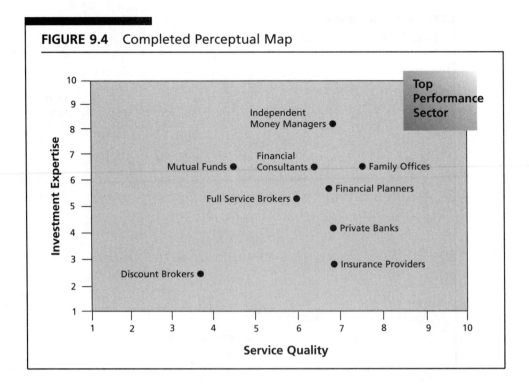

THE NINE LIVES OF THE AFFLUENT

The following nine profiles are psychological types of investors based on intensive interviews with hundreds of affluent individuals. A thorough understanding of these profiles is critical for dealing effectively with affluent investors—satisfying their need for customized, high-quality service and your desire to establish profitable, long-term relationships.

PROFILE 1: Family Stewards: "Good Investing Lets Me Take Good Care of My Family."

To Family Stewards, the primary goal of investing is to take care of their family. An investment representative wouldn't emphasize product but rather would talk about how the money would be managed in a way to meet the family's life cycle needs: education, retirement, travel, and so on.

Focus:

- Family Stewards are 20.7 percent of the HNW (high net worth) population, the largest of the nine profiles.
- $4.5 million is the average of invested assets per client.
- Successful investing enables stewards to provide and care for their family.

Motivation:

- Look for long-term results.
- Will trade off maximum returns for greater security.
- Talk about kids and their activities/sports.
- May voice concern about college funding/estate planning.

PROFILE 2: Investment Phobics: "The Last Thing I Ever Want to Talk about Is Investing Money."

Investment Phobics don't like the field of personal finance. In fact, they fear it. They are not knowledgeable about investing and dislike talking about it. A representative talking to an Investment Phobic should steer clear of the latest developments (derivatives, hedge funds, etc.) and definitely not enlarge on the nuts and bolts of investing.

Focus:

- 17 percent of the HNW population.
- $4 million average invested assets per client.
- Dislike discussing investments.
- Not knowledgeable about the markets and investing.

Motivation:

- They focus on personal rapport with their investment representative.
- They never broach subject of investing themselves.
- Investment representative should simplify concepts as well as provide support and reassurance.

PROFILE 3: Independents: "To Me, Successful Investing Means Freedom."

Independents are not always excited by investing but may even look on it as a necessary evil. But they will become involved, even highly involved, in the process if they think it necessary. For Independents, successful investing produces a sense of personal freedom and comfort as well as relief from financial concerns.

Focus:
- 12.9 percent of the HNW population.
- $2.8 million average invested assets per client.
- Consider focusing on investments a necessary evil.
- Consider personal security the benefit of wealth.

Motivation:
- Successful investing to Independents creates a sense of personal freedom.
- They regard investing as merely a means to a greater end.
- They discuss investing in terms of retiring early and a secure future.

PROFILE 4: The Anonymous: "My Money Is My Business and No One Else's."

The Anonymous prize confidentiality above all. They are secretive about all financial dealings. They see investment success as crucial to personal comfort and are quite concerned about possibly losing their money. Any presentation to this group would obviously emphasize the complete discretion of the investment representative in all dealings.

Focus:
- 11.8 percent of the HNW population.
- $5.6 million average invested assets per client.
- Confidentiality concerning investments prime.
- Secretive about all financial dealings.

Motivation:

- Need their representatives to show they understand the need for complete confidentiality.
- Reward brokers who understand them with loyalty.
- Very risk adverse and not knowledgeable about investing.

PROFILE 5: Moguls: "Being Rich Means Power."

Moguls see investing as a way of keeping score. More specifically, they see successful results as a way of gaining power and influence within a certain social environment. An investment representative talking to a Mogul should bear in mind that presentation is an important element to this particular profile.

Focus:

- 10.1 percent of the HNW population.
- $3 million average invested assets per client.
- Investing equals money, and money equals power.
- See investing as a way of keeping score.

Motivation:

- They drop names of political or social power figures.
- Control and influence are important to Moguls.
- Successful sales to Moguls must acknowledge their role in strategic decisions and need for control.

PROFILE 6: VIP's: "There Are Lots of Ways to Get Respect, and Investing Well Is One of Them."

The VIPs want the social recognition and prestige they can get from successful investing. They also see it as a way of keeping score. Among the nine profiles, keeping up with the Joneses will be most important to this group.

Focus:

- 8.4 percent of the HNW population.

- $4.3 million average invested assets per client.
- Highly materialistic and status conscious.
- Think successful investing results in being well known.

Motivation:
- Prestige and respect are important.
- Everything VIPs own looks expensive: their cars, watches, clothes, and so on.
- As with Moguls, money is a scorecard, but VIPs seek social status instead of power.

PROFILE 7: Accumulators: "You Can Never Be Too Rich or Too Thin. Thin Doesn't Matter; Rich Matters."

Accumulators just want to be rich. For them, money is very much a way of keeping score. However, they want the money as an end in itself and believe a person can never be too rich. The more they have, the better they feel, so their sole objective is to make more money.

Focus:
- 7.6 percent of the HNW population.
- $3.3 million average invested assets per client.
- Invest to make money and enjoy watching it grow.
- Believe a person can never be too rich.

Motivation:
- Often seek to maximize returns.
- Most interested in performance of any of the nine profiles.
- Not ostentatious and live well below their means.

PROFILE 8: Gamblers: "You Have Better Odds (Playing the Market) Than in Vegas."

Gamblers enjoy the process of investing and treat it as a hobby. They like playing the markets. They are more prone to having an active trading account. An investment representative could definitely focus on the details of an investment to hold the interest of the Gambler.

Focus:
- 6 percent of the HNW population.
- $3.8 million average invested assets per client.
- Relish the process of investing.
- Treat investing as a hobby.

Motivation:
- Derive pleasure from playing the markets.
- Like to work with brokers in choosing investments.
- Somewhat self-directed about their investments but recognize the value of professional representatives.

PROFILE 9: Innovators: "Derivatives Were the Best Thing to Happen to Investors."

Investors see investing as an intellectual challenge. This means they want to know the latest and most sophisticated approaches to investing. They keep current with the financial markets and learn about what's new in investment opportunities. In essence, they are the opposite of Investment Phobics.

Focus:
- 5.5 percent of the sample.
- $6.2 million average invested assets per client, the highest of the nine profiles.
- See investing as an intellectual challenge.
- Attuned to changes affecting the financial markets.

Motivation:
- Desire to be at the cutting edge of investing.
- Always looking for new technologies, tools, and investments.
- Most challenging group to serve because of high knowledge level. and potentially the most rewarding.

Which Clients Do You Want?

Early in your investment career you probably would have done handstands and flips for any of the preceding affluent personalities. But as your client base grows and your business matures, you may find yourself weeding out certain personalities that cause you more grief than gain. Some personalities are a perfect fit for your style and therefore are a pleasure to work with. Others, however, may be your worst nightmare come to life. Start deciding today what type of client you want to build your business around. You may be a highly versatile individual and can play any role required for these nine profiles. Or you may be someone whose stomach churns in the presence of certain profiles, and you'd rather just avoid them.

There are a couple of those affluent types that I have worked with that just drive me crazy. The flashy VIP who's wearing the gaudy jewelry, driving the latest, greatest car, and has to brag about his or her latest status purchase. I just want to hurl. I used to try to be amused by it but their egos drove me crazy. I decided to build my business around people I could connect with—Family Stewards, Independents, and so on. Another type that I had to avoid were the control freaks—Moguls—who think they know everything about everything and who just annoy you after awhile.

STEVEN J., BROKER

SYSTEM FOR IDENTIFYING YOUR CLIENTS AS ONE OF THE NINE PROFILES

Many investment advisors have requested some sort of checklist to help them figure out who's a Family Steward, who's an Investment Phobic, and so on. The following method, developed with and field tested by top producers, is called the Profile Diagnostic System (PDS). Basically, the PDS is a series of open-ended questions to ask your client that, by the process of elimination, helps you zero in on the exact profile of a client.

The PDS is comprised of four opening questions as well as a few follow-up ones. You probably already ask questions like these when working with your clients. However, what's different here is that the nine profiles give you something completely new to listen for. What makes this system work is not so much the questions themselves but rather learning to listen to your client's answer for the unmistakable traits of one of the nine profiles. You don't have to ask all the questions in the PDS—just as many as you need. It may take only one to get an idea of a client's profile, or it may take all four and a follow-up. It will vary by client. Go through the questions and note what you should listen for from each.

PDS Questions

- "What would you like your investments to achieve?" *Follow-up question:* Is it to take care of your family or to be more independent yourself?
- "When you think about your money, what concerns, needs or feeling come to mind?" *Follow-up question:* Are you more interested in accumulating it or in what it can do for you? And what can money do for you?
- "How involved do you like to be in the investing process?" *Follow-up question:* Is investing something you like to do, or have to do?
- "How important to you is the confidentiality of your financial affairs?" *Follow-up question:* Is there anyone else who needs to be in the loop on our investment planning decisions?
- "What would you like your investments to achieve?" This question quickly exposes two types—Family Stewards and Independents.

  Family Stewards are affluent investors whose primary motivation is to protect their family in every way possible, including financially. Family Stewards are often owners of businesses and tend to keep a lot of assets in their business so the enterprise can provide employment and a future for many family members. Family Stewards are very forward looking and are as concerned about the education of their grandchildren as helping their children with down payments on their houses. So if you ask this question of a Family Steward, you'll hear all about what they would like their money to do for their family.

  Independents will answer this question at the other extreme. Independents seek just what their profile implies—personal independence. Independents dream about chucking it all and sailing off into the sunset. Their portfolio buys them personal autonomy, the thing they value above all else. If you ask this question of an Independent, you won't hear about their family very much, if at all. You will hear about the dream house on the golf course, or sailing around the world, or being able to retire at 55. Listen carefully, though, for the theme of freedom and independence—not about material possessions, like boats, vacation homes, or similar things.

- "When you think about your money, what concerns, needs, or feelings come to mind? This question will help you identify Accumulators, Moguls, and VIPs.

  The key word *accumulate* will smoke out Accumulators. They are more financially savvy than most of the other groups. They are singularly focused on just one goal—accumulating more assets. Accumulators are not particularly concerned with what can be done with their money, just driven to accumulate it. Hence, their answer will be something like, "I just want my money to grow as quickly and safely as possible."

Moguls and VIPs are interested in money because of what it can do for them. Moguls value money for the power it gives them. They like to control people and environments. More money enables Moguls to have things more their own way. They tell stories of affiliations and friendships with power figures, like influential politicians, who are not necessarily famous. Also, Moguls see themselves as power figures, even minicelebrities holding considerable authority in their family, business, and community. Listen for these common themes from Moguls.

VIPs are status oriented. They like to be recognized and acknowledged. They like prestigious surroundings and trophy possessions. They tell stories about encounters with celebrities and often have pictures with them on their walls. They are interested in what money can do for them, but their examples will focus on material possessions: a wonderful new house, fabulous trips, or a new boat. VIPs invest for what it can buy and the lifestyle it can confer.

- "How involved do you like to be in the investing process?" This question is extremely effective in identifying Investment Phobics, Gamblers, and Innovators.

  Investment Phobics dislike investing; they are scared of it and highly intimidated by it. When you ask them a question like this, you will hear a lot about how much they don't like investing, how they are burdened by it, and that it's one more thing they have to do or worry about—or they'll attempt to change the subject completely.

  Ask this question of a Gambler or an Innovator and you'll hear enthusiasm and commitment. They like, even love, investing. Gamblers and Innovators are by far the most knowledgeable and expert of all, and this knowledge will come across in their answers. Listen closely to tell the difference between Gamblers and Innovators. Gamblers live and breathe investing. It's their hobby and sometimes their life. Gamblers love the thrill of market volatility.

  Innovators are not taken by the thrill of investing but by the intellectual challenge of it. They are technically sophisticated and like to be at the frontier or cutting edge of the investing world.

- "How important to you is the confidentiality of your financial affairs? This question is designed to identify one particular group—the Anonymous.

  The Anonymous are fearful and worried about personal security and confidentiality. They need constant assurance that you are protecting their information as well as their investments. They are moderately knowledgeable about understanding their investments. Ask this question of the other types, and you won't get much of a response. Sure, they want their dealings to be confidential, but they are not rabid about the issue. In contrast, the Anonymous are. They will explain how central this concern is to them and how essential it is in any advisory relationship. (See Figure 9.5, "The Profile Diagnostic System at Work.")

FIGURE 9.5 The Profile Diagnostic System at Work

Q: "What Would You Like Your Investments to Achieve?"

A: "Well, I just want my money to grow."

1. Family Stewards
2. ~~Investment Phobics~~
3. Independents
4. ~~Anonymous~~
5. Moguls

6. VIPs
7. Accumulators
8. ~~Gamblers~~
9. ~~Innovators~~

(Explanation: Client wants growth. This eliminates #2, 4, 8, and 9. But "why" do they want their money to grow? For their family, freedom, power, a yacht, or just to accumulate? A follow-up question is needed to clarify the motivation, and the profile.)

Q: "Are you more interested in accumulating it or in what it can do for you?

A: "I'm fairly frugal, don't spend a lot. I just like watching it grow and grow."

1. ~~Family Stewards~~
2. ~~Investment Phobics~~
3. ~~Independents~~
4. ~~Anonymous~~
5. ~~Moguls~~

6. ~~VIPs~~
7. Accumulators
8. ~~Gamblers~~
9. ~~Innovators~~

(Explanation: Client said he is frugal, eliminating VIPs. Client made no mention of family, power, or freedom, elminating all but Accumulator. Client said he enjoys watching the money grow. This confirms he is an Accumulator.)

Trial Balloons

Once you believe you know which profile a client may be, consider floating a trial balloon to see if you are on target. This way, you can confirm your hunch and proceed accordingly. Or disprove it early and avoid a misdiagnosis.

Creating and floating trial balloons is relatively easy. Simply follow the process in this flowchart. (See Figure 9.6, "Ideas for Trial Balloons.")

Example: If you thought someone was an Accumulator, you might say, "After having had a chance to get to know you, it seems to me that you are very astute about money. You know how to save it and how to make it grow. I enjoy working with clients like you and I'm going to do my best to make sure we create an investment strategy to make the most money possible."

Sample Trial Balloons

Family Steward: "It seems your family's well-being is your primary concern. We're going to create a portfolio that's focused on your family, that's going to really take care of them long term."

Investment Phobics: "I get the feeling you're not that comfortable with investing. But that's OK because I am, and I'm going to do my best to make sure that your goals are met so that you don't have to worry."

Independents: "It's really important to you to have the investment resources in the bank to make sure you have the freedom to do whatever you want. Maybe retire at 55. Maybe sail around the world. My job is to help you have that freedom."

The Anonymous: "You operate similarly to the way I work with my clients. My key concern is that confidential information stays confidential. When we work together, you can rest assured that confidentiality is one of my highest priorities."

Moguls: "I feel that you should be in complete control. My job is to make sure that you have the best advice and information in order to make the big decisions."

VIPs: "It's important that you know we work with some of the biggest names in the investment management industry—people at the same level as you. People who know and understand the appropriate investments for someone in your position."

Accumulators: "It seems to me that you are very astute about money. You know how to save it and how to make it grow. I enjoy working with clients like you and I'm going to do my best to make sure we create an investment strategy to make the most money possible."

Gamblers: "Investing is exciting for you, just as it is for me. I love everything about investing. Whether it's finding a great stock, watching CEOs on CNBC, or

FIGURE 9.6 Ideas for Trial Balloons

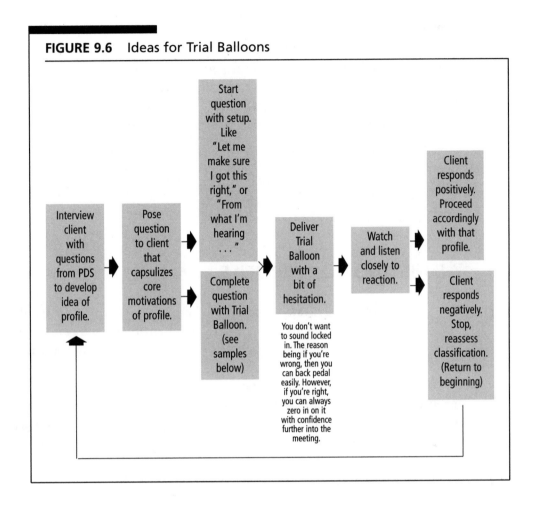

doing research on financials. Together, we can make sure we keep up with all of the events going on."

Innovators: "You have a great deal of knowledge about investing, and it's very important to you to use state-of-the-art investment approaches. That's precisely what my firm, and I in particular, specialize in."

It's clear that relationship factors are critically important to the satisfaction of your clients and the ultimate success of your business. However, how do you improve them? Clues can be found in *The Nine Lives of the Affluent.* Each of the nine profiles provides you with key insights into a client's motivations and goals. By understanding the profiles better, you can easily identify service points to improve on and deliver them more consistently.

Key Motivations for Investing
- **Family Stewards:** Taking care of my family
- **Phobics:** Last thing I want to talk about
- **Independents:** Means freedom
- **The Anonymous:** Nobody's business but mine
- **Moguls:** Means power
- **VIPs:** Gets me toys/status/respect
- **Accumulators:** To get rich and richer and richer
- **Gamblers:** Exciting and provides a hobby
- **Innovators:** Technical and mental challenge

ADJUSTING TO A PROFILE

Family Stewards are motivated to invest by the goal of securing their family's future. You simply need to think about how client orientation could benefit a Family Steward. To help, the following provides specific ideas on how to approach affluent clients.

The first element of client orientation is time management. It's a good idea to meet with the client at a time that doesn't conflict with a family activity, like a daughter's volleyball game or quality time at home together. Simply ask the client, "Is there a time we could meet that doesn't intrude on your family time?" By so doing, you indicate to your client that you understand his or her priorities and are willing to accommodate them, thereby increasing your client's satisfaction.

PROFILE 1: Family Stewards
(INCLUDE PHOTO)

Client Orientation:
- Involve key family members.
- Remember family occasions.

Keys for Leading:
- Emphasize experience in working with family issues.
- When talking about performance, stress reassurance.

Attending Behaviors:
- Schedule regular face-to-face meetings.
- Arrange meetings so they follow a regular, predictable pattern.

Shared Values:
- Share the importance of your own family in your life.
- Show how your value of thrift benefits the family.

When seeking to strengthen your relationship with Family Stewards, it's important to tie your activities, work, and conversations into the familial motivation. We found brokers/advisors accomplishing this in several creative ways. One broker sponsored a family day outing to the ballpark for his family-centered clients. There were lots of extra perks thrown into the day for the kids (hat, treats, etc.). Another advisor would comb the local paper every day for notes or stories about the sports and extracurricular activities of his clients' children. He would clip out an article and send it to his client with a note of congratulation. Still another broker had a connection in the Louisville Slugger plant and would get personalized bats inscribed with the name of clients' children ($35) to give to clients, making clients look like heroes.

PROFILE 2: Investment Phobics
(INCLUDE PHOTO)

Client Orientation:
- Avoid technical discussions.
- Learn a lot about their outside interests.

Keys for Leading:
- Encourage client trust by talking about perfectionism.
- Frequently inform them of high-quality performance, but don't spend a lot of time on it.

Attending Behaviors:
- Schedule fewer meetings.
- Meetings focus on lifestyle (not financial) issues.

Shared Values:
- Show interest in their life.
- Talk about your belief that investing is necessary but that not everyone has to be an expert.

Investment Phobics have little interest in talking investments and investment options. They want to be assured of your professionalism and expertise and need assurance that they are proceeding as planned. The relationship with Investment Phobics should center more on learning about their interests and lifestyle and probing into what changes or activities are occurring. They need assurance that you are keenly interested in their life, not just their money. You want to give simple, nontechnical overviews of their investment performance and try to communicate a sense that their confidence in you is being rewarded. The Investment Phobic feels stress when pondering financial matters. Work to allay that stress and to shield them from it.

PROFILE 3: Independents
(INCLUDE PHOTO)

Client Orientation:
- Be task driven and focused on client goals.
- Avoid technical discussions irrelevant to a client's goals.

Keys for Leading:
- Always talk about investment performance in the context of the client's main goal—financial freedom.
- Talk about successful experiences in working with similar clients.

Attending Behaviors:
- Provide frequent updates on the progress toward the goal of financial independence.
- Provide a periodic review of the financial objective.

Shared Values:
- Tell stories about other clients who have lived out their dreams.
- Talk about how appealing you think the idea of financial freedom is.

Independents are goal-driven, self-motivated individuals. Independents like to talk about their career, their goals, and their current progress in reaching their ultimate goal, which is freedom to do what they want with their time. There is strong drive in this goal-oriented personality. Independents want to work with an advisor who demonstrates the same kind of drive for success. They want to hear stories about others whom you've assisted in their quest for independence. Remember to continually show progress toward their ultimate goal. Independent individuals need the emotional assurance that they are one more day, one more quarter, or one more year closer to early retirement.

PROFILE 4: The Anonymous
(INCLUDE PHOTO)

Client Orientation:
- Give much attention to client privacy needs.
- Talk about firm commitment to client confidentiality.

Keys for Leading:
- Explore client preferences for maintaining privacy.
- Tell client about the firm's security procedures.

Attending Behaviors:
- You need fewer meetings than with most clients.
- Plan a short agenda because of time constraints.

Shared Values:
- Agree that privacy is increasingly important.
- Say you like working with clients who understand the need for confidentiality.

Privacy is the catchword with the Anonymous investor. The Anonymous needs constant assurance that you and your firm are discreet and protective of client information. The Anonymous investor requires less time and attention than the other profiles. When you do meet, your emphasis should be on demonstrating sophistication and professionalism and answering any questions the client may have. Remember that The Anonymous are risk averse and not particularly knowledgeable about investing. The Anonymous are second only to Innovators in average net worth ($5.6 million average invested assets). The Anonymous are more worried about losing money than about competitive returns. Your emotional keys are assurances of worth, preservation, and confidentiality in all matters.

PROFILE 5: Moguls
(INCLUDE PHOTO)

Client Orientation:
- Reinforce perception of client control at all opportunities.
- Create decision points for clients (opportunities to make decisions among several options).

Keys for Leading:
- Make them feel as though each is the #1 client.
- Make them feel as though they are working with the #1 firm in terms of investment performance and service.

Attending Behaviors:
- Meetings are organized around decisions they are asked to make.
- Reinforce previous client decisions.

Shared Values:
- Show that you think their accomplishments are significant.
- Set up choices for clients; don't question their decisions.

Remember the words *control* and *ego* with the Mogul personality. Unlike the VIP personality that craves attention and recognition, Moguls crave control and deference. They think highly of their own abilities to reason and decide. Moguls often think of themselves as experts in many areas, including investments. Moguls see themselves as power brokers and consider investing as a way of keeping score. Moguls believe that their investment success will result in increased leverage and community influence. A broker or advisor is engaged by a Mogul to explore options and uncover investment possibilities. The broker/advisor lays these options in front of the Mogul and awaits his or her judgment.

Emotional keys are the connection to social/political power figures and meeting their perceived need to be in control. One broker kept in touch with the important fund-raisers of his Mogul client's political party and bought tickets to these events, sometimes prearranging an introduction to an important figure at the event. This played well to his Mogul clients' need to be seen as influential.

PROFILE 6: VIPs
(INCLUDE PHOTO)

Client Orientation:
- Provide first class treatment (boardroom, best restaurants).
- Give the sense of many people involved on their behalf.

Keys for Leading:
- Make them feel as though they are in the same class as celebrity clients.
- Stress the sterling image of the firm.

Attending Behaviors:
- Schedule frequent meetings to address their ego needs.
- Ensure that the meeting content is not exceedingly challenging.

Shared Values:
- Drop names of celebrity clients of the firm.
- Talk about highly visible people in the community.

VIPs want to get noticed, and they'll spend money to get that notice. Pay attention to the car they drive, the watch and clothes they wear, and ask about the things they've purchased. They wear these purchases like a Boy Scout wears his badges.

VIPs want both prestige and respect and will solicit that respect with materialistic flash. You score relational points by playing to this vanity. Take them to the best restaurant or golf club and introduce them to other "important" people. Treat VIPs like celebrities and don't be afraid to drop a few high profile names of clients that you work with. Don't do or say anything that would challenge their image or ego. Your emotional keys are paying attention to accomplishments and status, first-class presentation and treatment, and the assurance that everyone in your firm is working for them.

One broker told us that he lost a wealthy client who fit the VIP profile because he failed to recognize the ego needs of that client. The client came from a looked-down-on city and went to what was regarded as a second-rate school. The broker would jokingly remind this client of his roots, not realizing how much it aggravated him. This VIP client had something to prove to the world. The final straw for the client came when he drove up to the golf course in a brand new Porsche and his broker failed to comment. The client became upset and soon moved his assets elsewhere. Childish? Yes. Vain? Yes. Shallow? Yes. But many investment professionals have found that if you want a good relationship with a VIP, you must play to his ego and recognize the flash.

PROFILE 7: Accumulators
(INCLUDE PHOTO)

Client Orientation:
- Communicate a sense of urgency around financial performance.
- Involve their other professional advisors (lawyers, CPA, etc.).

Keys for Leading:
- Report frequently on superior performance compared with selected benchmarks.
- In every interaction, reinforce investment expertise.

Attending Behaviors:
- Conduct frequent meetings.
- Focus all meetings on portfolio results.

Shared Values:
- Reinforce the value of accumulating wealth.
- Show your belief that private wealth is what made this country great.

Think of Accumulators as accounts that are never satisfied, wallets or purses that are never full. The emotional trigger may be the fear of not having enough or the greed of needing to have more today than they had yesterday. Accumulators feel a sense of urgency. They want growth. They want proof that their portfolio is growing. Give assurances to Accumulators that you are employing all possible resources (law, taxes) to ensure the growth of their resources. Accumulators want frequent communication and that communication needs to include a focus on the superiority of performance being delivered and an update on results. The Accumulators' "high" is seeing their money grow. You need to nurture that craving with good results and possibilities for superior performance relative to the general market.

PROFILE 8: Gamblers
(INCLUDE PHOTO)

Client Orientation:
- Communicate excitement and enthusiasm for investing.
- Ensure the highest possible interaction with the portfolio manager.

Keys for Leading:
- Emphasize expertise in taking advantage of market movements and volatility.
- Communicate trading versus a buy-and-hold orientation.

Attending Behaviors:
- Initiate many phone contacts between meetings.
- Quickly respond to clients' calls.

Shared Values:
- Mirror their emotional intensity.
- Show you share an appreciation for quickness, risk taking, and action.

Gamblers like action, energy, and excitement. They like to "play" with their money. Investments are a sophisticated means to a daily adrenaline rush. Many investment decisions by the Gambler have visceral rather than analytical foundations—that is, the chance to make a killing, make a score, or take advantage of the market's overreaction or ignorance. Gamblers derive much pleasure from action and want to work with brokers who can uncover trading opportunities. Your emotional keys are the excitement and enthusiasm you communicate about investing, an opportunistic attitude toward the market, and quick and frequent calls to Gambler clients. If you can't match their intensity, they'll find someone who will.

PROFILE 9: Innovators
(INCLUDE PHOTO)

Client Orientation:
- They want access to top technical expertise.
- Position yourself as an educational resource.

Keys for Leading:
- Bring leading-edge investment opportunities to these clients.
- Talk the technical jargon.

Attending Behaviors:
- Have frequent interactions (not just meetings).
- Focus on industry news and new products.

Shared Values:
- Share the belief that innovative, cutting-edge investing is the way to go.
- Reflect their technical turn of mind.

The Innovator is a challenge to any broker or advisor other than the well-seasoned, highly experienced, and extremely knowledgeable sort. Innovators dedicate much of their time to studying the markets and investment strategies—and they have the wealth to prove it. Of the nine affluent profiles, they are #1 in average invested assets—$6.2 million—even though they are the smallest group (5.5 percent).

Innovators want to use the broker/advisor for expertise, information, and cutting-edge opportunity. Emotional keys with Innovators are to be forward looking, to "talk the talk" of investments, to stay up on new trends, and to communicate often. Just as Gamblers challenge your energy level, so Innovators will challenge your knowledge and skill level.

Your affluent clients are no different than any other clients from the standpoint that you must find the emotional touchstones that drive their decision-making process. The profiles outlined here are a way for you to connect with the affluent investor on a relational and core-emotional level. Such an approach takes you to a deeper level with your clients because you will connect with the forces that motivate them.

Where do you fit in these profiles of the affluent? What are your key motivations? If others were trying to sell a product to you, would it help them to understand psychological and emotional characteristics about you? Of course it would. Psychographic information like *The Nine Lives of the Affluent* gives you an easy method for tailoring your services to the motivations that drive your client. Or as *Nine Lives* author Russ Prince put it, "Discover the emotional motivator that drove these individuals to build their wealth and you have found *the* key to helping them manage their wealth."

10 | Telling the Story of the 65+

Men resemble their times more than they do their fathers.

ANCIENT PROVERB

Many years ago I would look at older clients and think all the wrong thoughts. "They're going to be high-maintenance, nervous, and meddlesome. They are going to see their assets disintegrated by health problems. Their earning years are past and they'll die in a few more years anyway." I wanted the ambitious 35 to 50-year-olds with high incomes and lofty investment dreams. My, how my attitude has changed! My clientele today is dominated by retirees who have large portfolios and many good years ahead of them. If I were starting in the business today, I would fix my focus on those 60 years old and older and not look back.

RALPH L., BROKER

Not only is the mature market growing, but the assets of this group are growing as well. Future success in investment services hinges in large part on an individual's ability to build a sizable mature clientele. Consider these facts:

- Today there are over 31 million Americans aged 65 and older. This is roughly the same population as in the state of California. By the year 2025, the Census Bureau projects that number will grow to 63 million, which is equal to the population of California, New York, and Texas combined.
- One in seven Americans is currently over age 65. By the year 2025, that number will grow to one in four.
- The elderly population is growing 26 times faster than younger segments.

Today's retiree can expect to live longer. In 1960 the average American enjoyed a three-year retirement. Today's retirees have 20 years or more ahead of them, which means two decades of your helping them meet their financial needs.

Just how wealthy is the 65+ investor? Would you believe four times wealthier than the average investor aged 55 through 64 or nine times wealthier than the average investor aged 45 through 54?

Figure 10.1 shows the disparity of wealth between generations. The 65+ investor dominates with an average net worth of $485,000 compared with $121,000 for ages 55 through 64 and $54,900 for ages 45 through 54. In fact, the median net worth of older households exceeds that of all other segments combined! Mature

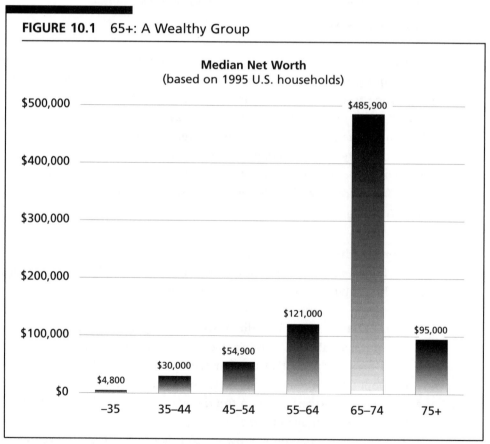

FIGURE 10.1   65+: A Wealthy Group

Source: Federal Reserve. Based on incomes of $100,000 and up.

clients own their own home and account for 40 percent of the country's total demand for goods and services.

It may take a little more work to find and keep a mature client but not as much work as it would take to service four 55-year-old clients or nine 45-year-old clients. That's how many average clients from those age groups that you'd need to equal the assets under management of one mature client. Simple math says that if you want to build a business, mature is better. Here's a little food for thought: How much will that $485,000 portfolio be worth in 10, 15, and 20 years? (See Figure 10.2.)

How do you adjust your communication when presenting to a 70-year-old client in contrast to a 40-year-old client? We're not referring to the investment strategy you offer or the products you promote but rather the values you focus on and the emotional touchstones you turn.

Will the 55-year-old in the year 2001 be guided by the same moral and emotional criteria as the 55-year-old in 1991? Absolutely not! The 55-year-old in 2001

FIGURE 10.2   A $485,000 Portfolio

Here's how $485,000 invested at 8 percent will have grown over the years:

- After 10 years: $1,047,079
- After 15 years: $1,538,502
- After 20 years: $2,260,564

That same $485,000 invested at 10 percent will have grown thus:

- After 10 years: $1,257,965
- After 15 years: $2,025,965
- After 20 years: $3,262,837

And at 12 percent, a $485,000 investment will have grown to:

- After 10 years: $1,506,336
- After 15 years: $2,654,679
- After 20 years: $4,678,452

How do you adjust your communication when presenting to a 70-year-old client in contrast to a 40-year-old client? We're not referring to the investment strategy you offer or the products you promote but rather the values you focus on and the emotional triggers you pull.

will be the first of the baby boomers (born between 1946 and 1964) whose attitudes toward the age they're approaching and the retirement they're nearing are psychological light years away from the 55-year-old in 1991.

The generations—the matures, boomers, and, for that matter, the Gen-Xers—all require an idiosyncratic understanding and approach because of their varying beliefs, attitudes, and experiences regarding the world they were formed in and the money that keeps it turning. Members of a generation are connected by the mutual life experiences in their formative years. The economies, politics, disasters, victories, technological strides, and cultural developments are some of the generational bonds that define these respective generations.

Marketers of any product error gravely if they believe they can offer their wares to any of these age groups with a common approach and focus. The primary issue for you as the broker or advisor is not what makes the investment product salable but what attitude or value in the 65-, 50-, or 35-year-old you can connect with that product.

The goal of this chapter is to sift through the defining values and attitudes of the mature generations to see how they differ from those of other generations and to guide you in the process of telling a "generational story" that connects your products and services to your clients' generational ethos. Today's 65+ investors are the richest demographic in history (average $485,000 in assets).

The following chart, borrowed from *Rocking the Ages* by J. Walker Smith and Ann Clurman of Yankelovich Partners, Inc., illustrates differences between these three generations at a glance (See Figure 10.3). Not only do values vary from generation to generation but so do motivations, purposes, and habits with money. The successful broker has learned to synergize the client before presenting a plan or product. Don't make the mistake of believing there's a definition of selling that translates equally to these three generational groups.

For example, all three groups indicate that they desire simplicity in their business dealings, but each group has a unique way of defining that simplicity. To mature clients, simplicity is predicated on accessibility. They want an advisor who is there for them, available to answer questions and ready to respond.

To boomers, simplicity hinges on efficiency. They want the best results with the least possible effort. Their life is busy and stressed enough. They want systematic and expeditious models for achieving their goals.

FIGURE 10.3 Generations at a Glance

	The Mature	Boomers	Xers
Defining Idea . . .	Duty	Individuality	Diversity
Celebrating . . .	Victory	Youth	Savvy
Success because . . .	Fought hard and won	Were born, therefore should be a winner	Have two jobs
Style . . .	Team player	Self-absorbed	Entrepreneur
Rewards because . . .	"You've earned it"	"You deserve it"	"You need it"
Work is . . .	An inevitable obligation	An exciting adventure	A difficult challenge
Surprises in Life . . .	Some good, some bad	All good	Avoid it—all bad
Leisure is . . .	Reward for hard work	The point of life	Relief
Education is . . .	A dream	A birthright	A way to get ahead
Future . . .	Rainy day to work for	"Now" is more important	Uncertain but manageable
Managing Money . . .	Save	Spend	Hedge
Program . . .	Social program	Cult deprogrammers	Software programs
Generational Film . . .	*The Best Years of Our Lives*	*The Big Chill*	*Reality Bites*

Source: from *Rocking the Ages*

For Gen-Xers, simplicity is defined by practicality. They want practical, useful products and services. Their eye is on the bottom line. They are averse to hard selling and very savvy about the manipulations of sales and marketing. They need practical reasons for using a broker's services rather than investing on their own.

Our goal here is to

- highlight the key values of the mature generation you must connect with to win its trust;
- review the life and cultural experiences that helped form its investing habits and attitudes; and
- address the "age-justments" necessary for your business to excel with this group.

WHAT IS AN "AGE-JUSTMENT"?

People change as they age. That simple fact is the reason we must consciously "age-just" our approach to the generation of the client before us. Clients make mental notes about our office, our style, our presentation, and our relational competency. The matures, boomers, and Xers are each looking for different features in a broker/advisor. The smart advisor recognizes the subtle "age-justments" necessary to positively impress the mature client and allows his or her speech and approach to reflect those adjustments.

Age-justments can affect everything from how to serve a cup of coffee to after-market strategies. The generational idiosyncrasies highlighted here will cause you to take a second look at your printed materials, your discovery process, and even your business card. This chapter includes practical, usable age-justments you can make immediately in your business.

You must learn to see the world as the older consumer does.

KEN DYCHTWALD

A highly successful broker working with retirees in Florida told us that working with mature clients is intense and demanding work and not to be underestimated. In fact, he said that it's like driving in a car at 100 m.p.h.—one sharp nudge on the steering wheel and you can flip your car. There is simply no margin for error. This experienced broker warns young brokers, many of whom think a client meeting with a 70-year-old is a walk in the park, to think seriously about preparation for meeting with a mature client. If the mature client senses any "disconnection" in values, needs or motives, the broker has effectively flipped the car.

Three fundamental principles for succeeding with mature clients are:

1. Preparation that embraces their physical changes
2. A presentation that embraces their psychological changes
3. A relationship that embraces the social changes

Preparation: You must do an age audit of your entire business—your literature, your office, your questions, your presentation style, and your follow-up service.

Presentation: How many times have you found yourself in the sales process with a 65+ client and the look on the client's face says she doesn't get it? The 65+ individuals are changing—and your presentation must change if you want to get their attention and keep their interest.

Relationship: In order to effectively compete for a mature client, it's important to emphasize building relationships as much as building assets. Studies show that as people age they care less about the product and more about the person delivering that product. To the 35-year-old you are selling performance, but to the 70-year-old client you are selling yourself.

GETTING PREPARED: AGE-JUSTING YOUR BUSINESS

Accept one simple fact, age-just to it, and you will succeed with any market: people change with age. (See Figure 10.4.)

What were you like 20 years ago? What will you be like 20 years from now? Are you wearing glasses or contacts today? Were you wearing them 20 years ago? Have you seen your ideologies shift as a result of your experiences, your children, or your incomes? Have you seen your eating and drinking habits change? At 20 we were eating burgers and pizza and drinking beer. At 40 we're eating

FIGURE 10.4   The Three Stages of Man

chicken and drinking chardonnay. At 60 we may be eating bran flakes and drinking prune juice.

At 20 we were driving a "beater" and praying that it would start and make it from point A to point B. At 40 we're driving a minivan with gummy worms stuck to the upholstery. At 65 our primary mode of transport could be a golf cart.

Everything changes as we age. Do our advisory businesses keep tabs on, and keep pace with, these age-related changes? For most the answer is no. The also-ran broker/advisor takes a myopic view of clients and gives a monotonous product-centered presentation to all clients irrespective of age. On the other hand, successful brokers/advisors have learned that age-related issues, concerns, values, and world views need to be noted, respected, and catered to. With the mature client, do it or else.

There are three fundamental shifts we must understand regarding the 65+ client—physical, psychological, and sociological. The materials we use and the offices we use them in must accommodate the physical changes. Our presentations must be "wired" to connect with the psychological changes, and our level of service and resulting referral business are tied to the sociological changes.

George Burns was once asked how people could tell if they were going from being elderly to old. He answered, "You know you're old when everything hurts and what doesn't hurt doesn't work. When your favorite part of the newspaper is "25 Years Ago Today," when friends stand around your birthday cake to keep warm, when you stoop down to tie your shoelaces and ask yourself, 'What else can I do while I'm down here?'"

Aging does have it's physical consequences. A simple way to understand these changes is to realize that at 65 your horizons are beginning to constrict:

- You can't see as far.
- You can't hear as well.
- You can't go as far (without difficulty).

Eye fact. By the age of 60, 93 percent of Americans will wear corrective lenses. This, of course, affects the way you communicate through print and should also affect the choices you make in selecting visual aids and literature for your older clients. Following are suggestions for your print communications;

- Use large type (at least 12-point) and choose a serif over a nonserif typeface. This is a 12-point serif type. This is an 8 point sans serif type.
- Be generous with the amount of white space on printed materials.

- Avoid reversing out large sections of type from a dark background.
- Use textured, matte paper rather than glossy, glare-producing paper.
- Minimize the use of light and italic typefaces. *This is italic type.*
- Make charts and graphs as simple and straightforward as possible.

Sounding off. Many people in the 65+ age group have trouble distinguishing background noise from your voice during a conversation. They may also have trouble hearing soft-pitched or high-pitched voices. Following are some suggestions for your vocal communications:

- Eliminate background noise during presentations.
- When calling your mature clients, allow the phone to ring eight to ten times to give them sufficient time to reach it (many older clients may not have voice mail).
- Speak more loudly and slowly and use lower voice pitches.
- Sit right next to your clients during face-to-face meetings. Try to avoid sitting across a large desk or conference table from them.

We found one broker who would perform a subtle hearing diagnostic with elderly clients. When he first started talking, he would drop his voice a bit. If any of his clients leaned forward or cupped their ears, he knew that they were having hearing problems. He thought this worked better than yelling, "Can you hear me?"

Mobility facts. Mature consumer studies show that there are four basic types of mature consumers who fall under the headings of extroverted and introverted: George Mochis, author of *An Aging Population,* speaks of the young/old and the old/old. The old/old are those who started acting their age long before they reached it.

In the extroverted aging population, Mochis describes healthy indulgers (13 percent) and ailing outgoers (34 percent). (See Figure 10.5.) These are categories of the aging population we can expect to grow as more and more mature people pursue the philosophy of you're as young as you feel. They are guided by the sentiment that Satchel Paige expressed, "How old would you be if you didn't know how old you were?" With people like John Glenn (78 in 2000) going in space and George Bush (73 in 2000) jumping out of an airplane, the mature population has seen its peers live courageous, daring lives that defy age. This aging population dares to go where no aging population has gone before. It will require sound financial advice to be able to confidently pursue its adventures and travels.

FIGURE 10.5 The Young/Old and the Old/Old

	Extroverted	**Introverted**
In Good Health:	Healthy Indulgers (13%)	Healthy Hermits (38%)
In Poor Health:	Ailing Outgoers (34%) 	Frail Recluses (15%) 

The mature who are in ailing health face a constant deterioration of their financial well-being with the threats of rising health care and drug costs. These costs take a major mature client's retirement income. Medicare covers one-half—sound planning will have to cover the other half.

There are some practical age-justments you need to make in your office because of the decreased mobility of mature clients. Many suffer from arthritis, hip replacements, and ailing knees and ankles. Some complaints we heard from mature clients included:

- "I wish they had a door you could push instead of a doorknob."
- "I can't turn the knob with my arthritis."
- "The chair was so soft it was hard for me to get out of it!"

Impressing mature clients and making them comfortable in our offices can start with simple adjustments like age-friendly door handles, chairs, floor coverings, or anything else that could affect mature mobility. This sort of age customization is on its way to becoming the marketing focus of the next decade as the 65+ age group continues to grow at unprecedented rates.

For example, General Motors' new Chevrolet Impala will have the ignition on the dashboard because engineers and consultants found that slightly arthritic hands could turn a key sideways more easily if the wrist was not already bent. The new Ford Focus will have door openings that will extend farther forward at knee level to make it easier for older drivers to swing their knees into the car. The new Cadillac Deville, which is a favorite of affluent mature clients, will have night vision technology that decreases the drivers' reaction time from 17 to 3 seconds.

It is important to make the age-justment as invisible as possible so there is no stigma attached. For example, an age-justment that hasn't worked out particularly well is large-print books. For many mature people, large-print books carry a stigma of being for old people. Mature clients want the customization without having to admit they're getting old. It seems that the mature person would rather wear bifocals, trifocals, or even "Coke bottle" glasses than carry around large-print books.

There is an age-defiant attitude prevalent among many of the 65+ clientele. You will meet those who believe you're as young as you feel or think. "How old would you be if you didn't know how old you were?" Many 70-year-olds would be 35. Many 35-year-olds would be 70. It is important to not only connect with the wisdom and experience of your 65+ clients but with their vigor and energy for life as well. You can treat them with respect without treating them as old.

CONDUCTING THE AGE AUDIT

We discovered that many advisors were making a lot of little age-justments that make a big impression on 65+ clients. Your office should be a setting that helps your 65+ clients feel at home. Following are some ideas we picked up from advisors who excel in the 65+ market. We have divided these ideas into two categories: easy (adjustments you can control) and structural (design and furnishings).

Easy Age-Justments

- Serve coffee in porcelain mugs rather than styrofoam cups. Styrofoam is cheap—and an environmental no-no—not the message you want to send your clients. Even some fast-food restaurants have discovered that porcelain coffee mugs lend a feeling of home and help return business among seniors. One advisor had a mug made for all of his 65+ clients with their name inscribed. All these mugs were hanging on a rack behind his desk. His theory was that he wanted every client to feel important and to feel like a friend.

- Provide treats such as homemade cookies and *soft* candy.
- Provide cookbooks for reading. Yes, you read that right. One advisor found that cookbooks were extremely popular with the 65+ crowd in his reception area because they provided a "homey" feeling.
- Get a bigger business card. We met an advisor in Florida who found that his 65+ clients couldn't read his card and therefore didn't keep it on hand. He then redesigned the card to make it 42 percent larger and easier to read—and noticed a significant difference in business.
- Provide family pictures and wisdom plaques. Many 65+ clients told us that they are comforted when they see pictures of the advisor's family; many like to ask about the family. Others mentioned being impressed but somewhat intimidated if there were too many credential plaques on the walls. Try a balance of credentials and a plaque with a wise saying that might reveal your values to the client.
- Be aware of your seating arrangement. For a more personal touch, move from sitting behind your desk to a round table with chairs. Sit close enough to the 65+ client to communicate friendliness and a neighborly approach. Don't seat 65+ clients facing a window where outdoor glare could agitate their eyes.

Structural Age-Justments

- Chairs. Make sure that your chairs are not so soft and cushy that a mature client struggles to get out. A firm, comfortable chair will suffice.
- Signage. Is your sign easy to read? Avoid reversed text, provide plenty of contrast, and use an easily read font.
- Door handles. Remember the complaint about arthritic hands struggling to turn a doorknob? Door handles that you push or pull down easily are preferable.
- Flooring. The rule of thumb for the 65+ is to have flooring that is not too thick or too slick. They may have trouble with thick carpet or fall on slick flooring.
- Lights. Opt for soft, natural lighting. Avoid fluorescent lighting wherever possible. Florescent lights often cause headaches and eye irritation. For a little more money, there are tube lights available that imitate natural lighting.

THE 65+ PRESENTATION

Once you have made the necessary physical age-justments in your materials, office, and approach, you are ready to make a presentation to 65+ clients in a voice and manner that suggests that you are aware of their needs, respect their experience, and understand their limitations. To be successful with 65+ clients, you must understand the cognitive shifts that have taken place in the mature. To effectively motivate this group, it is important to understand how the elderly mind differs from the youthful mind.

I try to never ask my elderly clients any questions that require them to recall numbers, accounts, or percentages. I noticed that when I did ask a number of specific questions in times past that many of them would have trouble recalling and would become flustered. I decided I didn't want any clients feeling frustrated because of a question I asked. Now I just ask them who I can call to get such information.

DUANE C., ADVISOR

This advisor intuitively adjusted his presentation to accommodate one of the major psychological shifts of the 65+ client, which is short-term memory loss. If you were to give a series of 24 nonsequential numbers to a 65-year-old and a 35-year-old and ask them to recall as many numbers as possible, the average 35-year-old would be able to recall 14 and the 65-year-old would recall 8.

Often an 80-year-old who can't remember a number he heard 60 seconds earlier can give vivid details of something that happened 60 years ago. This is the reason you want to focus on experiences with the mature client and not on statistics.

Ironically, although short-term memory is shifting, for most the long-term memory is intact. Often an 80-year-old who can't remember a number he heard 60 seconds earlier can give vivid details of something that happened 60 years ago. This is the reason you want to focus on experiences with the mature client and not on statistics.

When we are young, we rely more heavily on an analytical or left-brain process because we are absorbing information that is new to us. By the age of 60, our brain contains about four times more information than at age 20. At this point we make our decisions based not solely on new information but on a lifetime of stored memories and experiences. By pulling from our past, we have shifted our thinking to a right-brain process, which involves more subjective, conceptual, and visual decision making.

What does this cognitive shift mean to you as an investment advisor? It means that a just-the-facts approach won't truly motivate mature clients. They're looking for investment advice that teaches them visually, imaginatively, and, most important, relates to their past experiences. The illustrations, anecdotes, and metaphors we share in Chapters 12 and 13 are especially appealing to mature clients. Study them and use them in your presentations. Note how such illustrative material raises mature clients' interest level during your presentation.

SELLING THE SIZZLE

Surely you're familiar with the old sales cliché, "Sell the sizzle, not the steak." Older investors will tend to look at the facts (the steak) only after they have been attracted by an emotional appeal (the sizzle). And, more important, the emotional lead-in has to be relevant to each individual. It's up to you to do the detective work to uncover each client's unique touchstone and then use that touchstone to tie in with what you're selling.

Reason guides but a small part of man, and that the least interesting. The rest obeys feeling true or false, and passion, good or bad.

JOSEPH ROUX

I once had this 75-year-old client who would not diversify his portfolio with equities no mater how much evidence I showed him. He was OK with owning bonds, annuities, CDs, land, anything but stocks. I showed him historical charts to try to assure him but to no avail. Exasperated, I finally asked, "What do you have against stocks?" His answer, "Soup lines. My family stood in soup lines. Stocks caused that." This guy was emotionally stuck in 1931. When I said, "stocks," he felt insecurity, loss, and hunger. I was amazed at how strong those emotions could be after all those years.

RON D., BROKER

The shift to right-brain thinking is more pronounced in mature clients because they become guided more by emotion and instinct than by reasoning and proof. For example, in explaining the significance of 100-point moves in the market, one broker draws on mature clients' memory bank and emotions with the following illustration:

How significant is a 100-point move in a market trading at over 10,000? In 1995 we saw just 2 100-point or greater moves. In 1996 there were 6. In 1997 there were 52 100-point moves in the market. Now it seems like it happens every other day. But what is a 100-point move in a market trading over 10,000? It's like a 30-point move in 1991 when the market was at 3,000. It's like a 10-point move in 1981 when the market was at roughly 1,000. It is exactly the same as a 1.5-point move in 1945 when the market was at 165. Did people get nervous in 1945 over a 1-point move in the market?

In 1945, if the market had shot up 9 points, a "fella" might have gone out and bought a new Packard (he shows them a picture of a '45 Packard). Today's 3-point move is far less significant than a 9-point move in 1945. It's all relative. Only the media should be concerned about 100- to 200-point moves in the market.

Now, that's excellent storyselling—and the Packard picture is just the frosting on the cake.

Figure 10.6 shows some of the contrasts between mature thinking and the thinking of younger adults. To help you tailor your sales message, it's important to know how right-brain thinking can affect purchasing decisions. Look at the glaring differences between what motivates the younger versus the more mature consumer.

I think I do a lot better with elderly clients because it feels more like a "Can I trust you?" meeting than "How much can you make for me?" I like spending time

FIGURE 10.6   Aged to Perfection

Mature Consumers Respond to More Personalized Messages

Mature Adults	Young Adults
Declining materialistic values	Highly materialistic values
More subjective	More objective
High sensitivity to context	Less sensitivity to context
Perceptions in shades of gray	Perceptions in black and white
More individualistic	More subordinated to others
Less price sensitive	More price sensitive
Complex ways of determining values	Simple ways of determining values
Whole-picture oriented	Detail oriented
Reliance on intuition	Reliance on logic

getting to know them and their background and painting a few broad brush strokes about what we'll do to meet their needs. I've also become keenly aware that their needs are more emotional than they are financial. This all fits my style better than trying to compete with unrealistic returns expectations that many younger clients have in their head.

NORTON L., ADVISOR

The reasons mature clients are buying have changed, so the way you sell must change as well. In Figure 10.7 we have listed the seven key characteristics of the 65+ customer and how they should affect your sales presentation.

FIGURE 10.7 Seven Key Characteristics of 65+ Clients

and how they should affect your sales presentation	
65+	**Your Presentation . . .**
1. Like to take time in making their decisions	Be patient. Encourage questions.
2. Aren't motivated to buy based on "bandwagon" approach	Don't push "hot" funds that everyone is buying. Stress how the fund can meet their needs.
3. More attuned to value than to price	Focus on how you provide value, service, and convenience that makes a sales charge worthwhile.
4. Like to try new things that enhance their lifestyle	Focus on investments and services that can improve quality of—and simplify—their life.
5. Look for relevance in their purchase decisions	Uncover their touchstones. Tie what you're selling to the benefit that interests them.
6. Like to socialize with peers and learn from one another's experiences	Focus on meetings, events, and seminars. They provide a great opportunity for networking and referrals with the 65+ clients.
7. Like to talk about their life histories—the greatest influence on who they are today	Use what you learn in discovery to personalize your sales message to their life experiences. Tie your product to the wisdom they have gained.

Here are some illustrations of how financial professionals have approached these 65+ selling techniques:

BE PATIENT. A broker in New York told us that he closes his meeting with the antithesis of the traditional close, which is "Sign now." He will say to the mature client, "Unless you have a pressing need to do something today, we typically like to meet back with you in a week so you can take your time to think over your options and so we as a staff can get together and discuss how we can best serve you. Does that sound OK to you?"

This broker told us that many of his peers thought he was nuts to put off the close of the sale but experience showed he was right. What he had communicated to clients was that he understood their need to think it over and that his staff were concerned about giving them the best service possible. In fact, clients are flattered to know that the broker's entire staff were going to sit down and discuss the situation. The broker told us that more often than not, once these sentiments are communicated, the clients will say to him, "Let's get started."

STAY AWAY FROM HOT IDEAS—STRESS THE FUND THAT MEETS THEIR NEEDS. Howard is an advisor who hits this issue head on. He takes a piece of paper and draws a zig-zag line (see Figure 10.8) and says, "Here's how I look at my job. I'm here to provide you with two things: income and piece of mind. It's enough of a challenge to remain healthy—none of us needs a financial plan that increases our blood pressure and stresses our health. This kind of return chart, which is what you get when you chase hot funds, is a stressful roller-coaster of jubilation and panic. I don't have any interest in that, how about you?"

The client responds, "No thanks."

Howard then draws another line on the page (see Figure 10.8) and says, "Here's how I work . . . I want to achieve financial progress without financial pandemonium. I want to achieve steady, consistent returns without the adrenaline rushes, high blood pressure, and sleepless nights. Notice how we arrived at the same place a few years down the road, but we just took a less dramatic route. So you have to ask yourself, 'Do I want drama or peace of mind?'" He then waits for the client's answer.

Client answers, "Peace of mind."

Howard continues, "All right then, let's find a fund with an approach that follows this philosophy." He then pulls out a fund chart that shows growth matching the second line he drew and lays it next to the illustration (Figure 10.8). The association is now made in the client's mind between that fund and peace of mind.

FOCUS ON VALUE, SERVICE, AND CONVENIENCE: THINGS THAT MAKE A SALES CHARGE WORTHWHILE. Sell price and returns, and

FIGURE 10.8 Funds and Peace of Mind

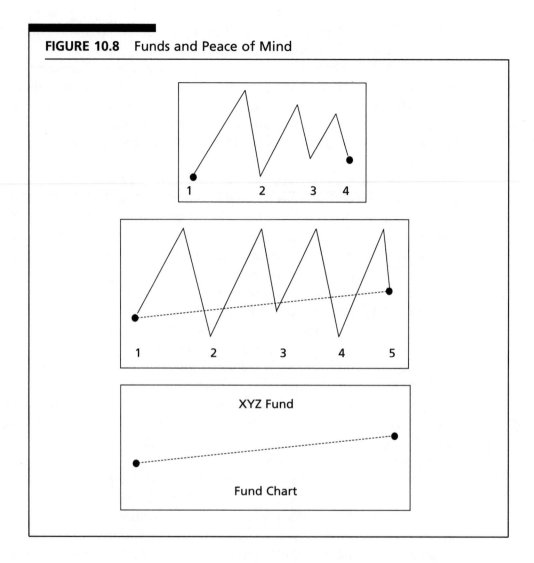

you'll lose. Sell relationships and service, and you'll win. It's that simple. The 65+ clients are more attuned to value than to price. Their minds desire a clear demonstration that you understand their needs and have a plan to meet them.

FOCUS ON SERVICES THAT SIMPLIFY THEIR LIFE. Everyone wants to simplify their life. One broker found a terrific analogy for communicating the idea of simplicity that is especially relevant to the 65+ set: the cruise control analogy.

Broker: "Mr. and Mrs. Jones, I know you like to travel. Let me ask you—do you use your cruise control when you're traveling?"

Client: "Sure."

Broker: "Most of us do because the cruise control gives us a margin of safety against speeding tickets and makes it easier to enjoy the ride because we have less concern about maintaining the right speed. Did you know that we have a way to put your income on cruise control? We put X in XYZ annuity and you're guaranteed a constant income stream for X years. You literally put your income on cruise control and have no concerns whatsoever about market fluctuations."

Storyselling is about using an analogy that is easily understood and tying it to a product that is not easily understood. Use the cruise control analogy to put your annuity business into overdrive!

TIE WHAT YOU'RE SELLING TO SOMETHING THAT INTERESTS THEM.

One day a retired client was telling me how his granddaughter had been showing him around the Internet and had talked him into getting a computer so they could stay in touch via e-mail. I could see my client was really intrigued by all this. I asked if he happened to notice what kind of computer she owned, what online service she used, and what Internet sites she visited. I suggested that some of these companies might be investment opportunities for him. He loved it! I could tell he felt like it was an investment in his granddaughter's world and that it was keeping him up-to-date with a changing world.

After this incident I decided to ask all my mature clients about the activities of their grandchildren as a tie-in to investment ideas. They are usually invigorated by the conversation and excited about the opportunities.

JOHN G., BROKER

What interests grandparents more than a grandchild? You can often get your mature clients to look to the future through the eyes of their grandchildren. That's a great storyselling approach. Try to tie every product you sell to something that interests the client, which is what we refer to as the "intrigue factor."

Find out what your clients' interests and hobbies are and sell them something related to it, which gives them something exciting to talk about with their friends over coffee. If your client likes to travel, find out how they travel. Is it in an RV, an airplane, or a cruise ship? Direct the client to a solid-performing related stock. If your client likes to golf, play tennis, fish, watch Nascar, or so on, have a conversation about which companies are prospering from these growing leisure trends and tie in an investment opportunity. If your client dotes on his grandchildren, ask him where he shops for them. For example, a high percentage of Toys 'R' Us sales are to grandparents.

One advisor, wanting mature clients to diversify into international funds, would ask about the products their grandchildren and children consumed and point out the global nature of those companies. He talks about their grandchildren drinking Nestlé Quik (Nestlé is a Swiss company), playing Sony and Nintendo video games from Japan, and wearing Fila shoes made in Italy. He also asks if their children happen to use cell phones (two-thirds come from Finland or Sweden) or drive European cars. These questions provide a highly relevant emotional link between the mature investor and international investments.

FOCUS ON MEETINGS AND EVENTS. The social life of a mature client is different from that of your younger clients. You need to be aware of and tie into two aspects of the mature client's social life:

1. Mature investors have more time to socialize with friends and thus peer influence becomes more pronounced.
2. Many mature investors are lonely and welcome opportunities to meet and mix with others.

Following are illustrations of how advisors have tied in with both aspects—that is, give the socializers something to talk about and the lonely something to do.

Further Ideas

Whenever one of her clients buys a mutual fund, Karen sends the client a fresh-baked pie. She attaches a note saying, "A mutual fund is a lot like a pie—no matter how big a slice you take, you still get the same ingredients. P.S. If you have any friends who need financial advice, feel free to give them my number." When asked why she sends a pie, Karen answers, "Because nobody eats a pie all alone. They're going to share it with someone and I'm trusting that my name will come up in the conversation." Judging by the number of referrals she gets, it's evident that Karen has found a recipe for success.

Pete, a lawyer turned advisor, told us the following story:

One truth I stumbled upon in dealing with mature clients is how terribly lonely some of them are. I find that many of them are searching for a breath of fresh friendship. I had a 77-year-old client, Ernie, who came in the office. We must have spent 15 minutes talking about small engines, which was his hobby. I also learned that Ernie had never been married and had no living relatives. He was truly alone. A week or two later my lawn mower broke and I thought, "I'll take this to Ernie."

You should have seen how glad he was to see me. He insisted on fixing it for free. Ernie and I now talk frequently and have formed a true friendship. I'm now much more sensitive to the loneliness of my mature clients.

How do you combine a big heart with marketing magic and help your business soar? Brent, a smart, big-hearted advisor decided to organize a Valentine's Day luncheon for his widowed clients. He figured that this was one day when widows are especially lonely and could use some friendly company. Brent puts on a first-class luncheon, gives flowers to each client, and invites all of them to bring a friend. Another advisor and author, Jerry Bennett, also focuses on widows. Jerry invites his widowed clients out for lunch for their birthday and invites them to bring five friends. He gets lots of clients that way and makes his current customer feel special (the client chooses the restaruant, by the way).

You can imagine the goodwill that Brent and Jerry have developed with those women and the good business that has followed. All they did was look for a real need, use some imagination, and meet the need with an event that clients would look forward to. Those steps are your formula for success in building your client base of mature investors.

DEALING WITH LOSS

One emotional phenomenon that we have found with affluent retirees is a condition we call loss of status syndrome, or LOSS for short. Former lawyers, executives, doctors, coaches, business owners, and star performers are now grappling emotionally with the sudden loss of status and control in their life.

Many have gone from telling scores of people what to do and when to do it to not being able to get a plumber to come to their retirement home for a repair. For much of their professional life, they were deferred to and saluted. Now, nobody knows who they are and, more important to them, who they were. Most have found retirement to be a disappointing mirage. How does all this affect you as a broker or advisor? Simply put, ask one question and you will win this retiree over—"What kind of work did you do?" Then, be prepared to listen. They may talk for a long time in order to relive the glory days. They want someone to be impressed again with who they are and what they did. They are hungry to again see the respect they worked so hard to gain.

Brokers have told us about so many clients who fit this loss-of-status syndrome profile:

- The former business owner who got up every morning at 3 AM, worked until 9 PM, built a very successful transportation company, and missed having people call him "Boss."
- The man who coached football at the collegiate and professional level and missed the training camps, the fresh prospects, and the publicity that went with the game.
- The former local media personality who was always stopped on the street and thought he was annoyed by it all—until he moved away and nobody stopped him anymore.
- The former CEO who said he now felt like a nobody amongst all the ex-CEOs in his retirement community.

Recently, in a *Newsweek* article, a retired lawyer talked about how difficult it was to go from being a respected head honcho with lots of control to just another retiree in a Florida community. Today he has trouble getting the lawn service guy to return his phone calls. Back in his working days, all he had to do was snap his fingers. Today he's looked at as just another grumpy retiree. That loss of status can be quite painful. Such people love to talk to the person who wants to know what they did and what they learned.

I'm finding as I've thrived and aged that much I'd thought was bad was good and what I thought was good was bad. I doubt I'd want to age again without the harmful fun I had.

ART BUCK

MOTIVATORS FOR THE MATURE

If the way a mature client buys changes, then the way we sell must change also. Motivations change as we age. According to a study of mature motivations, the four major motivators for the 65+ crowd are:

1. The need and concern for independence
2. Connection to family
3. Personal and spiritual growth
4. Rest and relaxation

I'm finding as I've thrived and aged that much I'd thought was bad was good and what I thought was good was bad. I doubt I'd want to age again without the harmful fun I had.

Note that mature investors are no longer motivated by growing assets. In many ways 65+ clients are the perfect clients. They're not looking to you to make them rich; they're looking to you to keep them from becoming poor. Your presentation to 65+ clients is about protecting what they have and maintaining their independence instead of growing their portfolio at 15 to 20 percent a year.

A philosophical shift takes place in the soul of the 65+. Money loses its power as a purpose and motivation. The mind of the 65+ becomes more emotional in nature and people grow in importance. The 65+ client is motivated to do things for family, church, and community. A smart advisor will focus on such issues as independence, family, altruism, and financing new experiences. Many in the age 65+ set are pursuing their personal growth through trying new adventures and going to places they've never been.

Make sure you are selling what the 65+ investor is buying. They are not buying hot funds, high returns, or long-term growth. The 65+ investors may be paying rent for independent living, financing gifts to family and community, and paying for adventure and R&R. Are these what you're selling? Are these the areas you're probing to pinpoint their interests and motivations?

I'm always amazed at how relational my meetings with mature clients are. So much of the meetings involve feeling me out to see if I understand them, to see if they can trust me. I don't think it does me any good to spend my time demonstrating how good I am at what I do—my track record and all that. They seem concerned with one question: "Do you understand my situation and my needs?" I can assure them just by asking the right questions and showing a sincere interest in them as individuals.

ROD M., ADVISOR

Given these requisites—means of existence, reasonable health, and an absorbing interest—those years beyond sixty can be the happiest and most satisfying of a lifetime.

ERNEST ELMO CALKINS

With maturity comes the wish to economize—to be more simple: maturity is the period when one finds the just measure.

BELA BARTOK

MATCHING VALUES

A true measure of your worth includes all the benefits others have gained from your success.

CULLEN HIGHTOWER

As Tom Browkaw so poignantly stated in his best-selling book *The Greatest Generation,* "This 65+ crowd is truly the greatest generation. This is a generation of people that has given much to its world, communities, and families. They are truly a generation worthy of honor."

It is important for you the advisor to understand the specific values that have guided this 65+ crowd and to match those values wherever you can. This is a generation that rebuilt from a depression, a dust bowl, and a world war. This generation learned to work together as soldiers, factory workers, union members, and citizens. Loyalty and patriotism were essential to making its world work. It developed a strong trust in institutions like government and big business. For this generation, conformity and fitting in have been linked to success.

This is a generation that understands the necessity and virtue of hard work. It preferred blood, sweat, and tears to education as a way to get ahead. This is a generation whose sense of self-sacrifice glorified duty over pleasure. It understands delayed self-gratification. It did much for its children, who got much of what *they* wanted. Hard work and sacrifice never seemed to fail.

The key values you want to highlight to the 65+ crowd are:

- Hard work
- Self-sacrifice
- Teamwork
- Honor for elders

We live in a society that seems to have lost the ideal of honor for the elderly. Once people reach a certain age, they are cast aside like societal refuse. The 65+ client was raised with a different set of mores toward the elder. Many mature clients took their aging parents in and cared for them. They believe in honoring their elders. They seem to sense when the person they're dealing with doesn't respect that value.

I must have taken my mother to a half dozen advisors/brokers until we found one we liked. Afterward, I started thinking about why we liked the one we picked. For me I believe the commandment to honor your father and mother is a lifelong commitment. I was looking for an advisor who would honor my mother as I do, someone who would care for her as though she were his or her own mother. When we sensed that kind of genuineness and concern, we stopped looking.

RICK H., CLIENT

Grow old along with me! The best is yet to be, the last of life, for which the first was made.

ROBERT BROWNING

11 | Telling the Woman's Story

Being a woman is a terribly difficult trade, since it consists principally of dealing with men.

JOSEPH CONRAD

How smart is it for a financial services professional to ignore 50 percent of all small business owners and 42 percent of the people with assets greater than $600,000? If you are not actively and purposefully pursuing the female investment market, this is exactly what you are doing. Look at these recent statistics:

- Forty-two percent of households with assets greater than $600,000 are headed by women.
- Women own one-half of all small businesses with a total of $8 million.
- Women earn more than one-half of all bachelor's and master's degrees.
- Ninety percent of all women will eventually be solely in charge of household finances.

Fifteen to 20 years ago, women may have been on the investment business radar but nothing like they are today. The only female clients many brokers had were the widows of their retiree clients. Not so these days. Women are asserting themselves economically and may be the most untapped opportunity for the financial industry today.

TUNE IN AND GET RICH

Today's financial services professional can build a fast and profitable book of business by tuning in to the female investor. One such advisor is David Bach, author of, *Smart Women Finish Rich.* Bach built himself into a multi-million-dollar producer in less than five years with a client base that is 80 percent women! David Bach is a model of the female-conscious advisor of tomorrow—a demographic you can't afford to ignore. Investment dollars are going through a phenomenal gender shift.

When asked how he became alerted to the community of female investors, Bach told us:

My wake-up call came when I started noticing that every other week we had someone dying. We were meeting with widows and trying to teach them about money at the worst possible time in their life. I thought this was all backwards. Why wait until tragic circumstances to teach a woman about financial management and investments?

I decided to develop a seminar just for women and to start addressing the wives of our clients while their husbands were still alive. When I first proposed the idea to my peers, they told me to leave the women to the women brokers. Now that I have over 150 million under management with female clients, they are no longer saying that.

For the first seminar I reserved a room that would hold 50 people and invited the wives of our clients—225 women showed up! The local newspaper did a full-page feature article, and the whole concept mushroomed. These women began to bring in an enormous number of referrals—and the business they brought was huge.

Bach states that many advisors allowed three myths prevent them from pursuing this female investment market:

Myth #1: The sales process takes longer with women than with men. Not true. Men may often be in more of a hurry, but if you explain things well, the process takes no longer with a woman.

Myth #2: Women are more emotional about investments than men. Not true. When properly educated about market fluctuations and the like, women are actually less impulsive, whimsical, and tempestuous than men.

Myth #3: Women are more conservative than men. Not true. Many of his 75-year-old clients are still caring for family members and seeking more aggressive investments.

Bach warns that once you pollute a relationship with women, you're done. This happens most often by talking only to the husband and not recognizing the wife as a source of information or as a decision maker.

For those who want to grow their business with women, Bach advises, "All the money eventually ends up in the woman's hands. If you're not solidifying the relationship with your client's wife, when he's gone you'll lose the account."

For those who want to grow their business with women, Bach advises, "All the money eventually ends up in the woman's hands. If you're not solidifying the relationship with your client's wife, when he's gone you'll lose the account."

This is a market you want to set your sights on and start working toward. "Aah, not so fast," we can hear some of you thinking, "if I know women, they would rather deal with a female investment professional. What chance do I have?"

The answer is a much better chance than you think. Seventy-eight percent of the women interviewed in one study conducted by Van Kampen Funds said that the gender of their financial advisor is unimportant to them.

"Yeah, but," we hear some of you staunch skeptics ruminating, "is there really that much money in the hands of that many women?"

How do these numbers strike you?

- Forty-seven percent of all women contribute regularly to a retirement account.
- Thirty-seven percent of all mutual fund assets are controlled by women.

I went to a broker and was so offended I decided I would learn to do everything on my own. I'm sure I'm making some mistakes that a professional could help me avoid but that man's attitude toward me was disturbing. I'm sure he is not representative of everyone in his field, but I won't sit through that again. He looked down his nose at me. He talked to me like I was a child. He did everything but call me "darlin'." I couldn't tell if he was being paternal or patronizing—or both. I almost felt like a teenager trying to prove I was an adult with my money. It wasn't anything he said. It was the body language and tone that said, "Oh, this poor little girl doesn't know what she's doing with her money." All I could think was, "How many men has he ever treated this way?!"

—NANCY S., CLIENT

We have witnessed many brokers/advisors in focus groups who don't have much regard for female investors. We have seen some who flippantly disregarded the female market as unproductive and unnecessary and others who, speaking with condescending and chauvinistic tones, dismissed consulting with women as a hassle.

These unenlightened individuals, while a minority, do give the entire industry a bad name.

We've witnessed other brokers/advisors who, desiring to gain more market share with female investors, didn't think there was any need to adjust their approach on the basis of sex. To quote one advisor, "People are people and money is money. People want to protect their assets and see their wealth grow. I don't see a whole lot of differences between the sexes on those issues."

This advisor's presumption of little difference between the sexes on issues of money is based on clients' goals and not clients' values. But if no values connection is made between the broker and the female client, there will be no opportunity to help her work toward her financial goals.

Mars, Venus, and Money

Advisors who adopt an androgynous approach toward their clients are operating in the dark ages of psychology. Scientific strides have been made to demonstrate clear and undeniable differentiations in the physiological and psychological systems of males and females. Scientists have found conclusive differences between men and women in every single system of the human body. Our bodies and minds are literally wired and designed to operate on different frequencies. If you are a male advisor, the fact that a woman's cardiovascular system functions differently from yours is of little concern, but the fact that her brain operates differently is of major concern.

David Bach did not build a multi-million-dollar investment business with female clients by treating them just like his male clients. Neither will you. Once you discover the female view of problems and how to apply solutions, you are on your way to building a gender-balanced and much richer book of business. In fact, if you're like David Bach, you may just decide it's more profitable to build your business around the female investor.

BETSY AND THE THREE BROKERS

Betsy is a recently divorced professional who suddenly found herself in need of a financial advisor. Betsy decided she would interview three brokers before deciding where to place her assets. Before she went to any interviews, Betsy determined specifically what it was she was looking for in a broker. Because customer service was important to her, that was the first thing she planned to gauge. Also, she wanted to be treated with respect and to be given the opportunity to grow.

With those three features in mind (customer service, respect, the opportunity to grow), Betsy went to see the first broker. She described him in this way:

He was playing the macho game, bragging about how great he was and how rich he was going to make me. He tried to impress me with all the "bells and whistles." He kept talking about his great software and great products. I tried to give him some personal information, but he showed no interest and just kept talking. He assumed that I was totally ignorant, which I'm not. I've got a lot to learn, but I do know a few things. Assuming that I am ignorant is one thing I just cannot tolerate.

Well, Betsy was off to a great start, wouldn't you say? This broker must have paid a lot of money for that software but somebody forgot to tell him that the client was more important than his software.

Betsy packed her portfolio and headed off to broker number two. She knew she was in trouble as soon as she crossed the threshold to his office. "Come in," he muttered, without looking up.

The entire time this guy didn't once make eye contact with me. I couldn't even think about my finances. I felt embarrassed. "What's wrong with me? Why won't he look at me?" I couldn't get out of there soon enough—and I don't remember a thing about the conversation.

Was broker number two such a successful guy that he didn't need to make eye contact, establish rapport, or even show respect? Was it an honor for a client to get an appointment with him? Or did he fail Communications 101?

Betsy, now duly unimpressed with financial services professionals as a whole, headed off to see broker number three. Little did this guy know that all he had to do was shut up, make eye contact, and he would get the business.

Fortunately for Betsy, broker number three not only made eye contact, but he focused his entire presentation on her needs and goals and never mentioned a word about software.

Betsy told us:

I saw right off he was a straight shooter. As soon as I sat down he started asking pertinent and critical questions. He inquired into my financial and life needs. He treated all my questions as very intelligent ones. I never got that look that says,

"You don't understand that?!" He really impressed me by giving me three different portfolio plans to choose from. He showed me the possibilities but let me choose! This is the respect and potential for personal growth I was looking for. Today he is my broker. And you know what? He's never too busy for me. He always has time to answer my questions. That kind of customer service tells me I have the right broker.

The female marketplace has one prominent parallel with the mature marketplace and that is the importance of relationships that bear results. Your relational ability is the key that determines whether your office becomes a resting place or a revolving door. Women shop for it and won't be satisfied in an advisor relationship without it.

Do you have the best record in town? She doesn't care. Do you have all the techno-gizmos to make investing easy? Don't bore her with it. The chief question is, "Are you comfortable being warm and relational with clients?" If not, don't even bother taking her appointment.

Do you have the best record in town? She doesn't care. Do you have all the techno-gizmos to make investing easy? Don't bore her with it. The chief question is, "Are you comfortable being warm and relational with clients?" If not, don't even bother taking her appointment. If you want to partake in the booming female investment market, it will require a conscious shift from the cold, hard, pragmatic results-driven male domain to the warmer, relational world of "getting to know their needs."

"WE NEED TO TALK"

Watch the fear those words evoke in the eyes of the average man. Those are the words he will hear when there are problems related to his Mars and Venus views of life. Those words are often spoken because there *are* significant differences between male and female thoughts, emotions, expectations, and communication styles.

Can you differentiate between male and female expectations of an advisor? Do you know what a female's major concerns are regarding the advisor relationship and how she wishes to communicate with her advisor?

First, let's take a look at the different expectations that females and males have for their advisors as shown in Figure 11.1. For women, the relationship is key. Most women need to feel they have a relationship with their advisor before they make a decision to hire one. "So what, does she have to date her financial advisor?" says he. No. But most women consider their relationship with their advisor

FIGURE 11.1

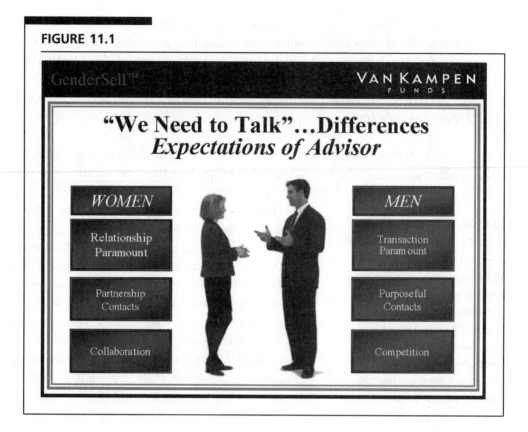

very significant—right up there with their therapist, spiritual advisor, or business partner.

Most men, on the other hand, just want to take care of business and complete the transaction. They are not concerned with having a relationship with their financial advisor. Most men feel they already have more relationships than they can handle. Sure, as men, we should like the person and he ought to have a good track record, maybe invite us for a golf game once in a while, but that's more than enough relationship for the average guy.

Some male advisors feel threatened by the word *relationship* and worry about what this might involve. However, what women are looking for is a financial advisor who will take the time to relate to their lives as a whole, not just to their finances.

Let's take a look at what the research says about this. Van Kampen Funds conducted research with the Opinion Research Corporation, interviewing hundreds of women investors. The survey covered such product and performance-oriented attributes as "gets me satisfactory returns" and "offers a wide range of product." Figure 11.2 shows the results of comparing the percentage of investors who attribute a 10 for importance to three relational traits.

What the study found is that there wasn't much difference at all in what men and women expected in terms of product and performance. There *was* a difference in what they were looking for in terms of the relationship. Women viewed the following three relational factors 20 to 30 percent more important than men:

- Listens to me
- Treats me with respect
- Keeps my best interests in mind

FIGURE 11.2

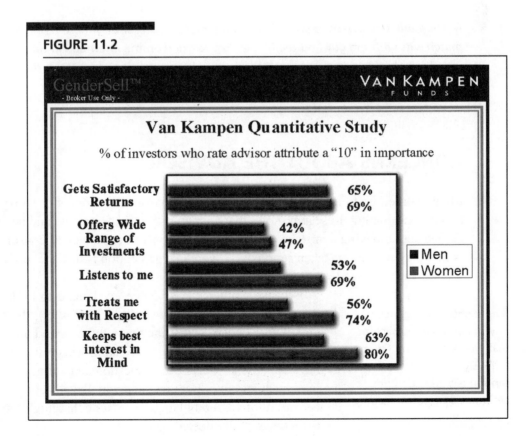

COLLABORATION OR COMPETITION

What many women ultimately want out of the relationship is a spirit of collaboration, the feeling that they're working with you toward a common goal.

Often for men, the meeting or decision is a competitive venture. One guy put it this way, "When I bought my car, from the minute I walked into the showroom, all I could think about was, 'I've got to stay on top of this deal,' or 'How much can I get him to come down on the price?'" I was not going to be beat.

Many men perceive the first meeting as a situation of win-lose. Often, they think they already know as much as the advisor and enjoy the competition of having more inside scoop than the advisor. Once they feel they've established the upper hand, they want to get down to business, take action, buy or sell. A man would rather say he needs an advisor because he's too busy rather than saying he doesn't know what he's doing. Sounds like an ego thing, doesn't it?

My husband and I went to see a broker and my husband's sitting there trying to match wits with the guy and tell him all he's learned on the Internet. I'm thinking, "If my husband knew as much as he thought, we wouldn't be here in the first place!" I just wanted to blurt out, "We need help, what can you do?"

CATHERINE T., CLIENT

CONCERNS ABOUT THE ADVISOR

Many women go to their first meeting with an advisor after months of worrying and procrastinating. Research shows that women may fear the process and be concerned about making a mistake. The number one concern of women as consumers is that they will not be taken seriously. A woman's perception is that she might be ignored or patronized.

The number one concern of women as consumers is that they will not be taken seriously. A woman's perception is that she might be ignored or patronized.

Because women's confidence levels tend to be lower than men's, (*Managing Diversity,* AARP 4/99), the second major concern is that they won't understand the concepts, the words, the theory of investing. This is the reason the wise advisor treats every question a client asks as an intelligent and important one and why the advisor should be careful of any body language or tone that might imply the woman really doesn't get it.

I'm no genius when it comes to investing, but that doesn't mean I'm not a smart person. I've got a graduate-level degree and am successful and knowledgeable in my profession. Advisors ought to respect the fact that maybe you know some things they don't and they know some things you don't. Nobody in this meeting is a fool; somebody is just better informed in the investment area.

RACHEL L., CLIENT

The last concern of typical female clients is that they will be taken advantage of. Many are afraid of being conned or duped in some way, so their radar is up—especially at the beginning of the relationship.

Taken to the Bank

Years ago after our father died, my mother invested a big chunk of money with a guy who promised great returns and a life happily ever after. Some of the money was put in a stock and some in a fund. The stock lost about 40 percent and the fund lost about 30 percent and the advisor never called. When my mother called, she found the advisor was no longer with the firm.

I have three sisters and they are now incredibly paranoid about anything investment related. The pain, the stress, the regret, and the anguish that we saw added to our mother's loneliness and grief were horrible. She was too trusting at the time. Now my sisters want me to be involved in everything for fear they'll end up going down the road that mother did.

VINCE L., CLIENT

Understanding the fear of vulnerability and of being taken should alert advisors to exercise patience in explaining options, to use a low-pressure approach to selling, and to deliver a realistic view of risk and return.

One advisor put it this way, "My women clients tend to view their assets as a static pool of water that will eventually be depleted, and men seem to view it as a dynamic river of assets that keeps flowing."

Talk the Talk

If you were to eavesdrop on a woman talking, it's doubtful you'd hear patter about business, money, and sports. Instead, you'd most likely hear conversation revolving around people, feelings, and relationships. What this means to you is that opening with small talk about sports, money, or business isn't going to sit so well with women. Women can go into a high-stress mode when they hear lots of financial jargon like PE ratio or nonqualified corporate retirement plan, especially when it's early in the relationship.

Your communication style needs to embrace the female preference for conversation. Figure 11.3 contrasts male and female communication styles and illustrates the fact that, with females, your aim is to communicate teamwork and facilitation.

TALKING FOR THE SAKE OF TALK

For men, communication is a means to an end—the end may be solving a problem, fixing something, or conveying information. And because of this, the facts are typically the most important thing. When it comes to an advisor relationship, again

FIGURE 11.3

the transaction, the exchange of information, the buying and selling, or the performance of the portfolio is what's important.

But for women, communication is an end in itself—the goal is to understand the other person and to be understood. For women, the connection is the main thing. And in an advisor relationship, having mutual understanding and rapport with the financial advisor is the focus. Because of this, women tend to be facilitative conversationalists.

Women are more likely to listen (and less likely to interrupt), ask more questions, and make sure there's a dialogue taking place and that the other person understands what's going on. They are more likely to nod, say "Uh-huh," and reflect on what the other person has said. The goal of a conversation for women is mutual understanding at the finish line!

The *structure* of communication is also different between the sexes (see Figure 11.4). Women tend to be very descriptive in their communication—and men tend to be very concise. Let's demonstrate:

FIGURE 11.4

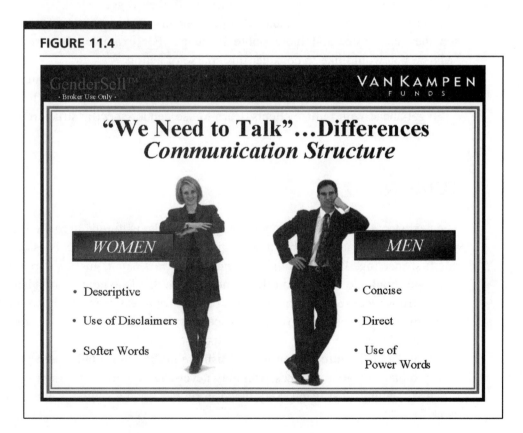

Ask a women to describe a man's shirt, and she might say, "It's fun and kind of approachable. It suggests that he puts some thought into his appearance and that he's friendly. I also like the color . . . it's a very peaceful blue."

On the other hand, the male might answer, "It's a golf shirt."

The female might respond, "That's it . . . a golf shirt? That tells me nothing."

The male might respond, "That tells you exactly what you need to know—it's a golf shirt. Most men don't have time for that 'peaceful blue' stuff."

Disclaimers

A woman might also seem to be apologizing for herself. But she's not—she's simply using disclaimers. Women often use disclaimers in their speech to couch what they're saying—usually for fear of offending someone else or not wanting to appear arrogant or superior.

Most men would never do that. Men say what they mean and mean what they say. They're direct. If someone is offended, well, they'll get over it.

But most women want to make other people comfortable. That's part of the reason they use softer and more polite language. For example, they might say, "Maybe you would like to consider this course of action."

But men like to use power words. Instead of saying, "Maybe you would like to consider this course of action," they would say, "Here's what you've got to do . . ."

To get ahead with female clients, learn to use gender-specific structure in your communication.

TUNE IN

The next step a man selling to a woman needs to take is to tune in to the message she is trying to send about her goals, values, and needs. Tuning in is essential at this first meeting. *What we basically mean is to just listen.* Just as important as what you should do is what you should not do, and that is to not interrupt her. People interrupt because they think that what they have to say is more important than what anyone else is saying. We can all see how annoying that is. Also, don't sell to her and don't offer advice unless she specifically asks.

Beyond a basic introduction to establish credibility, don't talk about yourself, your products, or your services. You may never even mention stocks or bonds in this first meeting. Just listen. Stay tuned in on her—same station, same channel, same focus!

One way to do this is by using active listening skills. This is probably the most important single skill that men can develop to improve communication with women. For example, if your client says, "I just don't have time to do half the things I want to," you would paraphrase her comments by saying, "Sounds like the time crunch is really a problem for you." She'll know you heard her.

THE VALUES LADDER

Another tune-in technique that is especially effective is something we've called the Values Ladder, which we got from David Bach, the million-dollar producer we mentioned earlier. He uses it with his female clients to gather information about their needs, goals, and values.

Bach starts off by asking his clients to focus on values. Of course, focusing on values is not the first thing that advisors typically talk to their clients about. Usually the focus is on returns. But when you think about it, money is not an end in itself. It's a tool to help clients achieve some particular end, something that's important to them. Women are usually very attuned to this. Research shows that today's consumer in general is more focused on quality-of-life issues, and that women in particular are especially receptive to focusing on values, spirituality, and simplifying their lives.

The way you want to start off is to ask, "What's important about money to you?" And their answers usually fall into two categories: goals and values.

Goals are tangible. They are usually related to specific things or experiences and have a specific monetary value. Buying a house or traveling are goals.

Values are intangible desires—the things in life that your clients really care most about. They carry no price tag. Freedom and greater spirituality are examples of values.

What you want to get your clients to focus on are values, because they're significant. If clients can get clear on their values, it will help them feel a sense of comfort and trust in you and it will help them make some decisions. So let's look at how to help them define these values by doing a Values Ladder. (*Yankelovich Monitor,* April 1999, About Women and Marketing, Information Access Company, January 1999.)(See Figure 11.5.)

In the Values Ladder approach, you can ask two specific questions: *"What's important about this?"* and *"Why is it important?"* You can continue to ask these questions throughout the interview.

An example is a 33-year-old woman named Jessica, who is married with a son and earns about $75,000 a year as a computer salesperson.

FIGURE 11.5

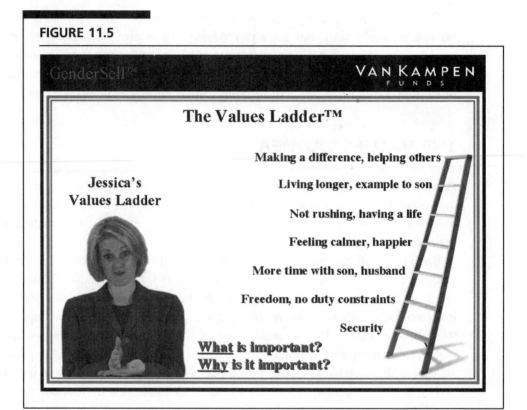

The advisor asked, "What's important about money to you?"

Jessica's answer was security. This is the first rung on her ladder.

But security means different things to different people. So the advisor asked, "What's important about security to you?"

For Jessica it meant that she could feel the freedom to do what she wants and not feel constrained by the duties of life—which became the second rung on her ladder.

So what's important about freedom? Jessica said that if she had more freedom, she would spend more time with her son, who was growing up very quickly, as well as with her husband and friends. This became the third rung on her ladder.

Her advisor went further and asked what would be important about having this time with her family and friends. She said she would feel calmer and happier, and that right now she felt burned out all the time—the fourth rung.

What's important about feeling calmer and happier? Jessica's answer was that, as it was, she spends so much time running around working, being a wife and mother, keeping the house in order, and so on that she doesn't feel she has a life and is exhausted all the time. Rushing and feeling like she had no life became the fifth rung on her ladder.

When Jessica was pressed to define why she wanted to have a life, she said she would take better care of herself, exercise, eat better, and so on so that she would live longer and be a better example to her son—the sixth rung.

And finally, what's important about having a better, longer life? It was tough for her to answer this one, but when she thought about it, Jessica realized that she would get more involved with charity groups in her community. Making a difference and giving something back were values for her. This became the seventh and final rung on the ladder. (From Van Kampen's "GenderSell" Program)

After she completed the ladder, Jessica realized that she really wanted to spend more time with her family, slow down, and, ideally, have time to do volunteer work in the community. What was she actually doing? Nothing even close to her values. She was working 60 hours a week, feeling pressured to make money, and spending most of her time in the office. And to top it all off, she was spending a great deal of money to finance her harried lifestyle.

After Jessica's advisor had gone through this exercise with her, he had established a foundation and uncovered her core motivator. He could now begin to build trust with her and develop an investing plan and portfolio to meet her needs.

It's a quick and effective tool to jump-start your relationship with any client—male or female—although women are usually more receptive to taking the time to do it. And it's a perfect way to tune in.

TEAM UP

The next thing men selling to women need to do is team up. What you want to do is form a partnership with each one. Most of the time, you should hold off on the presentation phase with women for a second meeting.

Talk to her in her language. Present at her level of knowledge—that is, don't talk over her head or go to the other extreme and oversimplify. It's good to say things like "As you may already know . . ." or "This can be a difficult concept to understand." Use brief stories or metaphors to convey your point. For example, you might talk about another client similar to your prospect and what she decided to do.

Another key thing to remember is to act in accord, although you do not need to sell your soul to do it. If she has investment ideas of her own, don't argue with her or tell her she's wrong. If a female client says it's important to her to buy stock in socially responsible companies, don't just say, "That's a bad idea." Better to say, "We can do that. Let's do some homework to find out which socially responsible companies are truly profitable."

And keep it interactive. Consistently check out where she is in the process by asking if you've been clear, if she has questions, and so on.

Women also tend to be more concerned about making mistakes in their investment decisions. So the more you can use objective data from outside credible sources (like Morningstar, Lipper, the financial press) the better.

LOCK ON

Finally, men selling to women need to lock on. You've finally reached the last stage, but don't get overzealous. You still will want to follow some of the principles we've talked about in the discovery and presentation stages. Your goal here is to cement the relationship. Some ideas:

- The most important thing to remember here is to take it easy. Don't push for the sale. Go very slow—you take much less risk that way.
- Keep in touch after the sale. More than men, women want to stay connected and to think that you are keeping them and their best interests in mind. Try to call your female clients every four to six weeks, even if it is only to leave a voice-mail message.
- Send her articles that may be related to her business or some other interest.
- Here's the clincher: *research shows that women are more likely to make referrals than men.* So if you stick with these principles, you'll establish a happy, satisfied client who is likely to send business your way. Keep in mind, though, that women are slower to trust. It's in your best interest to wait until things are going well before asking for a referral.
- Not only are women great at referrals, but your female clients will stay in their investments longer than the men and will stay with a broker longer if they're satisfied with the relationship.

Dr. Judith Tingley, author of *GenderSell—How to Sell to the Opposite Sex* and an expert on marketing financial services to women, tells of her own joy in finding a financial advisor who understood her gender-related needs:

I had interviewed a number of brokers/advisors until I found one that understood what I needed as a client and as a woman. His approach was simple but effective. First, he partnered with me—he would ask me what I thought about his suggestions. He also understood me and my business. He would often send me articles of interest that pertained to me and my work. We met twice a year in person and I felt like he cared about me. He had good follow-up even if he had nothing really important to say about my investments. I liked this advisor so much that I told many of my friends and colleagues about him. He paid attention to me and I sent business to him!

Are you starting to see a new powerful source of income here? We hope so. Serve women's investment needs sincerely and they will reward you richly.

PART FOUR

Let Me Tell You a Story

12 | The Metaphorical Magic of Warren Buffett

Warren's gift is being able to think ahead of the crowd, and it requires more than taking his aphorisms to heart to accomplish that—although Warren is full of aphorsims worth taking to heart.

BILL GATES

When Warren Buffett was once asked about the worst investment decision he ever made, he said, ironically, it was purchasing the firm his holding company is named after, Berkshire Hathaway. Buffett said, "We went into a terrible business because it was cheap. It's what I refer to as the 'used cigar butt' approach to investing. You see this cigar butt down there, it's soggy and terrible, but there's one puff left, and it's free. That's what Berkshire was when we bought it—it was selling below working capital—but it was a terrible, terrible mistake."

The cigar-butt metaphor about buying a bad business is vintage Warren Buffett. The story reveals much about Buffett's nonpretentious sense of gravity but also indicates what a master storyteller he is. Buffett would be an American icon even if he weren't a great communicator because he is so phenomenally rich (around $40 billion as of this writing, second only to Bill Gates). But the fact remains that Buffett is what we would call a master storyseller. He brings a Will Rogers-like delivery of irony, humor, simplicity, and common sense to a realm dominated by confusing analysts and economists.

Warren's gift is being able to think ahead of the crowd, and it requires more than taking his aphorisms to heart to accomplish that—although Warren is full of aphorsims worth taking to heart.

Americans have always simultaneously admired and resented their richest countrymen. Buffett seems to garner much admiration but escapes the accompanying resentment. We think some of that is due to his entertaining and illuminating delivery of plain talk and wisdom.

It also may be due to the fact that Americans save and channel their resentment toward the country's richest man, Bill Gates. While Gates is often seen as a modern monopolist, Buffett is viewed as the sagacious grandfather of investing insight.

Much has been made of the man who has been called the Oracle from Omaha, the Corn-Fed Capitalist, and the Forrest Gump of Finance. Untold books and articles have been written outlining his ideas and philosophies of investing. What we wish to draw your attention to is his ability to communicate—which is a big reason people like this plain-talking billionaire. The Berkshire Hathaway shareholders' meetings in Omaha have become a sort of capitalist's Woodstock. People want to hear what Warren has to say!

Buffett is not only smart, he speaks with simplicity. He doesn't talk over people's heads. Buffett is interesting and entertaining. He speaks with descriptive imagery that causes people to remember what he says. Buffett doesn't come off as self-inflated but rather as nonpretentious—maybe that's the advantage of working in Omaha instead of on Wall Street.

Enough has been written pointing to Warren Buffett as the model for investing. We include this chapter because we wish to point to Buffett as a model for communicating about investing. Not only has he been phenomenally successful as an investor, he has been incomparably successful at communicating investment truths with his "clients," the Berkshire Hathaway shareholders.

Warren has taught his clients well—they are in it for the long haul. Look up Berkshire Hathaway shares today to see how many traded hands. 100? 200? You may attribute it to the price of the stock or to his track record alone, but since when has a stock price or a good track record kept emotional investors from buying and selling? Buffett, through his letters and speeches, has done a remarkable job of communicating cornerstone truths about long-term investments.

How would you like to have a client base that focused only on the long term? How would you like clients who were no more concerned about market fluctuations than they are by 20 m.p.h. winds blowing outside their door? How would you like a book of business that invested with intellect instead of adrenal glands?

We think there is much to learn from the Oracle of Omaha about teaching long-term investment philosophies that you can apply to your business. We suspect that if you will simply imitate some of Warren's communication competence, your clients might begin to see the wisdom in what you are telling them. Go ahead and quote him; after all, who's going to argue investing philosophy with Warren Buffet?

Looking back to the used cigar butt story, we see that it reveals both the competence and style of this great investor-communicator. In that particular story we see the following:

- He tells it like it is. He is not afraid to admit to and talk about his mistakes and the lessons he learned from them. Are you comfortable enough with yourself to emulate him?
- His approach is simple. He doesn't try to dazzle people with complex talk about ratios, theories, and projections—although he understands them all. He speaks in a language *anybody* can understand. Can you simplify investment ideas to the point that the butcher and the baker know exactly what you're talking about?
- His metaphorical style is both illustrative and entertaining. If you can get clients to think, see a picture, and chuckle, you have made a significant psychological leap. Are you exercising metaphorical magic in your presentations?
- He keeps money and investing in proper perspective. As much as Buffett enjoys making money, he doesn't get caught up in the trappings of success. He enjoys the accumulation of wealth, not the demonstration of it. His sense of thrift inspires confidence in his investors. Does your approach to success and lifestyle inspire confidence and allegiance in your clients?

William Ruane, the founder of the Sequoia Fund, has this to say about Buffett's communication skills: "Warren is a genius, but he can explain something so simply and with such great clarity that, at least at that moment, you understand exactly what he's saying."

William Ruane, the founder of the Sequoia Fund, has this to say about Buffett's communication skills: "Warren is a genius, but he can explain something so simply and with such great clarity that, at least at that moment, you understand exactly what he's saying." (Janet Lowe, *Warren Buffett Speaks,* New York: John Wiley & Sons, 1998, p. 6.)

Let's take a closer look at Buffett the communicator. Familiarity with his wit, wisdom, and metaphors will greatly enrich your communications portfolio.

TELL IT LIKE IT IS

People appreciate plain talk. Buffett was once called Omaha's Plain Dealer because of his propensity for telling it like it is and his personal dearth of pretentiousness. He has never seemed to shy away from revealing his investment errors and what he learned from them. This attribute also inspires confidence in investors. In a rare public appearance with Bill Gates at the University of Washington, Buffett said:

I've made all kinds of bad decisions that cost us billions of dollars. They've been mistakes of omission rather than commission. I don't worry about not buying Microsoft, though, because I didn't understand that business. And I didn't understand Intel. But there are businesses I did understand. Fannie Mae was one that was within my circle of competence. I made a decision to buy it and just didn't execute. We could have made billions of dollars. But we didn't do it. Conventional accounting doesn't record that, but believe me, it happened. (Fortune, July 20)

Buffett has stated: "I've often felt there might be more to be gained by studying business failures than business successes. It's customary in business schools to study business successes. But my partner, Charles Munger, says all he wants to know is where he's going to die—so he won't ever go there." (Reported by Andrew Kirkpatric in "Of Permanent Value: The Story of Warren Buffett." Birmingham, ARDE, 1994.)

Buffett confessed that he finally bought Microsoft stock after Gates personally spent about seven hours explaining the business to him. Buffett confessed that he only bought 100 shares, "probably because I have an IQ of around 50." (*Fortune*, July 20) Yeah, right, Warren.

Warren Buffett seems to be smart enough to know that it is best not to become a part owner in a business that you don't understand. It can cause too much loss to own businesses that are Greek to you. Buffett owns Coke and Gillette because he says he understands colas and razor blades.

Clients want to know that you understand the businesses in which you invest their money. They want you to have enough understanding to inspire confidence for the long haul. How often have you seen doctors losing money in high-tech and high-tech engineers losing money in biotech? These people would have been better off to put their money into issues they understood. Instead, they chased rumors and hot tips.

Buffett is reputed to have said, "With a million bucks and a hot tip you can go broke in a year." This is what he refers to as investing with the glands instead of the intellect. Buffett is quoted in Forbes as saying, "Investment must be rational; if you can't understand it, don't do it." (Warren Edward Buffett, *Forbes 400,* October 21, 1991, p. 151) After selling some shares over 30 years ago, Buffett told the local paper, "I want to be able to explain my mistakes. This means I only do the things I completely understand" (*Omaha World-Herald*, December 5, 1968).

People are easily drawn into the adrenaline rush of media hype and rumored opportunities. Plain talk is the antidote for this emotional affliction. Buffett says, "Maybe the grapes from a little eight-acre vineyard in France are really the best in the whole world, but I have always had a suspicion that about 99 percent of it is in the telling and about 1 percent is in the drinking." (Janet Lowe, *Warren Buffett Speaks,* John Wiley & Sons, 1998, p. 36)

Charles Munger, Buffett's best friend and business partner, is also quite renowned for his plain talk. Munger says that promises of riches and grandeur don't impress much at Berkshire Hathaway. Regarding growth projections offered by companies, Munger states:

They are put together by people who have an interest in a particular outcome, have a subconscious bias, and [their] apparent precision makes them fallacious. They remind me of Mark Twain's saying, "A mine is a hole in the ground owned by a liar." Projections in America are often lies, although not intentional ones, but the worst kind because the forecaster often believes them himself. (Janet Lowe, Warren Buffett Speaks, New York: John Wiley & Sons, 1998, pp. 45–46.)

Acquainting yourself with the powerful and convincing metaphor of Mr. Market (see Chapter 3) that was invented by Buffett's mentor, Benjamin Graham, is one way that you can help your clients insulate their emotions against hype. Pretense is the saboteur of trust. Hype is the enemy of stability. Plain talk can help you establish both trust and stability with your clients.

DOES GRANDMA GET IT?

Use the Grandma test with all your communications. Are your explanations of investing concepts simple enough that any grandmother out there would understand the principle or idea you're talking about? If not, it's not Grandma's problem—it's your problem. Until you learn to simplify by saying, "It's kind of like . . ." you're going to find yourself explaining matters over and over and being met with perplexed stares.

With his investing genius, Buffett also possesses a gift for explaining investment matters with simplicity and clarity. What a combination of abilities! Sounds like a perfect blend of talents for a broker/advisor, doesn't it?

Follow Buffett's example and simplify everything you talk about. Every stock. Every fund. Every strategy and investment vehicle must be simplified to fit Grandma's

Follow Buffett's example and simplify everything you talk about. Every stock. Every fund. Every strategy and investment vehicle must be simplified to fit Grandma's lexicon and breadth of understanding. Confusing your audience does not cultivate trust.

lexicon and breadth of understanding. Confusing your audience does not cultivate trust.

Clients yearn for simplification and understanding. Scattered throughout the following are some Buffett simplifications: "All there is to investing is picking good stocks at good times and staying with them as long as they remain good companies." ("Warren Buffett Triples Profits," *New York Post,* May 14, 1994, p. D1)

Many clients tacitly worry that they're not smart enough to understand investing and the markets. But Buffett preaches that investing success does not run parallel with IQ: "You don't need a rocket scientist. Investing is not a game where the guy with the 160 IQ beats the guy with the 130 IQ." (Brett Duval Fromson "Are These the New Warren Buffetts?" *Fortune, 1990 Investors Guide,* p. 182)

What are the chief cornerstones of investing? Is it possible to simplify what it is that constitutes a great investment opportunity? Buffett believes there are. He states:

> I consider there to be three basic ideas, ideas that if they're really ground into your intellectual framework, I don't see how you could but do reasonably well in stocks. None of them are complicated. None of them take mathematical talent or anything of the sort. Benjamin Graham said:
> "1. You should look at stocks as small pieces of the business.
>   2. Look at market fluctuations as your friend rather than your enemy. Profit from folly rather than participate in it.
>   3. The three most important words of investing are margin of safety."
> Buffett went on to say that he "believes those ideas, 100 years from now, will be regarded as the three cornerstones of sound investing." (Buffett speech, N.Y. Society of Security Analysts, *December 6, 1994)*

We don't need to make things complicated. As one preacher said, "For God so loved the world that he didn't send a committee." Buffett too has a great religious analogy you might like to use that stresses the need for simplicity: "Value investing ideas seem so simple and commonplace. It seems like a waste to go to school and get a Ph.D. in economics. It's a little bit like spending eight years in divinity school and having someone tell you the Ten Commandments are all that matter." (Buffett speech, N.Y. Society of Security Analysts, December 6, 1996)

Would you like another simplicity metaphor with a biblical genesis? Here's another Buffett gem: "I can't be involved in 50 or 75 things. That's a Noah's ark way of investing—you end up with a zoo that way. I like to put meaningful amounts of money in a few things." (*The Wall Street Journal,* September 30, 1987, p. 17)

Buffett seems to believe that people often add excessive layers of complexity in choosing investments. When he's looking for a company to buy, he has some criteria he follows: earnings, earning power, debt ratio, management quality, attractive price, *and* simplicity. He wants simple businesses that are easy to understand. We believe this is what clients want as well. Simplicity leads to understanding and understanding leads to peace of mind. And peace of mind is the best return on investments you can offer your clients.

Buffett says it in this nugget of wisdom, "If principles can become dated, they're not principles." (Berkshire Hathaway Annual Meeting, Omaha, 1988)

METAPHORICAL MAGIC

We have arranged some of Buffett's best metaphors into a one-metaphor-per-page format so you can easily copy them for use in client presentations. The pictures and the metaphors are both important for triggering clients' imagination and emotion.

Some of these analogies deal with business and money, and some deal with life in general. We think you'll find them all to be very useful in moving clients toward common sense. Feel free to make copies for "show-and-sell" purposes in your client presentations.

BUFFETT ON YOUR GREATEST THREAT TO ACCRUING WEALTH . . .

"The arithmetic makes it plain that inflation is a far more devastating tax than anything that has been enacted by our legislature. The inflation tax has a fantastic ability to simply consume capital. It makes no difference to a widow with her savings in a 5 percent passbook account whether she pays 100 percent income tax on her interest income during a period of zero inflation or pays no income taxes during years of 5 percent inflation. Either way, she is 'taxed' in a manner that leaves her no real income whatsoever. Any money she spends comes right out of capital. She would find outrageous a 120 percent income tax but doesn't seem to notice that 5 percent inflation is the economic equivalent."

(Warren E. Buffett, "How Inflation Swindles the Investor," Fortune, *May 5, 1977, p. 250)*

Investing for the Long Run

BUFFETT ON TAKING
THE LONG VIEW . . .

"I buy on the assumption that they could close the market the next day and not reopen it for five years."

(Omaha World Herald, *July 31, 1983*)

"You could be somewhere where the mail was delayed three weeks and do just fine investing."

(Linda Coraut, *"Striking Out at Wall Street,"* US News and World Report, *June 20, 1994, p. 58*)

Investing for the Long Run

BUFFETT ON WEATHERING UPS AND DOWNS . . .

"In any business, there are going to be all kinds of factors that happen next week, next month, next year, and so forth. But the really important thing is to be in the right business. The classic case is Coca-Cola, which went public in 1919. They initially sold stock at $40 a share. The next year, it went down to $19. Sugar prices had changed pretty dramatically after World War I. So you would have lost half of your money one year later if you'd bought the stock when it first came public; but if you owned that share today—and had reinvested all of your dividends—it would be worth about $1.8 million. We have had depressions. We have had wars. Sugar prices have gone up and down. A million things have happened. How much more fruitful is it for us to think about whether the product is likely to sustain itself and its economics than to try to be questioning whether to jump in or out of the stock?"

(Berkshire Hathaway Annual Meeting, Omaha, 1992)

Investment Principles

BUFFETT ON THE DIFFERENCE BETWEEN POPULARITY AND VALUE . . .

"In the short run the market is a voting machine; in the long run, it's a weighing machine."

(Forbes, *November 1, 1974*)

"Most people get interested in stocks when everyone else is. The time to get interested is when no one else is. You can't buy what is popular and do well."

(Ann Hughey, Omaha's Plain Dealer, Newsweek, *April 1, 1985, p. 56*)

Investment Principles

BUFFETT ON INVESTING VERSUS GAMBLING . . .

"The propensity to gamble is always increased by a large prize versus a small entry fee, no matter how poor the true odds may be. That's why Las Vegas casinos advertise big jackpots and why state lotteries headline big prizes.

People would rather be promised a [presumably] winning lottery ticket next week than an opportunity to get rich slowly."

(Janet Lowe, "Warren Buffett Speaks," John Wiley & Sons, 1998, p. 106)

Investment Principles

BUFFETT ON HANDICAPPING STOCKS . . .

"There are speed handicappers and class handicappers. The speed handicapper says you try and figure out how fast the horse can run. The class handicapper says a $10,000 horse will beat a $6,000 horse. [Ben] Graham said, 'Buy any stock cheap enough and it will work.' That was a speed handicapper. And other people said, 'Buy the best company and it will work.' That's class handicapping."

(L. J. Davis, "Buffett Takes Stock," N.Y. Times Magazine, April 1, 1990)

Investment Principles

BUFFETT ON THE TYPES OF COMPANIES YOU WANT TO INVEST IN . . .

"Wonderful castles, surrounded by deep, dangerous moats where the leader inside is an honest and decent person. Preferably, the castle gets its strength from the genius inside; the moat is permanent and acts as a powerful deterrent to those considering an attack; and inside, the leader makes gold but doesn't keep it all for himself. Roughly translated, we like great companies with dominant positions, whose franchise is hard to duplicate and has tremendous staying power or some permanence to it."

(Berkshire Hathaway Annual Meeting, Omaha, May 1, 1995)

Irrational Investors

BUFFETT ON DUMB REASONS TO BUY . . .

"For some reason, people take their cues from price action rather than from values. What doesn't work is when you start doing things that you don't understand or because they worked last week for somebody else. The dumbest reason in the world to buy a stock is because it's going up."

(L. J. Davis, "Buffett Talks Stock," The N.Y. Times Magazine, *April 1, 1990, p. 16)*

Life Principles

BUFFETT ON THE IMPORTANCE OF GOOD HABITS . . .

"The chains of habit are too light to be felt until they are too heavy to be broken . . . you will have the habits 20 years from now that you decide to put into practice today. So I suggest you look at the behavior that you admire in others and make those your own habits."

(Fortune, *July 20, 1998)*

Life Principles

BUFFETT ON GETTING THE COMPETITIVE EDGE . . .

"I would say a lot of things in business really have the same effect as if you went to a parade and the band started coming down the street and all of a sudden you stood up on tiptoe. In another 30 seconds everybody else is on tiptoe, and it would be hell on your legs and you still wouldn't be seeing any better. The real trick is to stand up on tiptoe and not have anyone notice you."

(Fortune, *July 20, 1998*)

Life Principles

BUFFETT ON DOING WHAT YOU LOVE . . .

"My guess is that if Ted Williams was getting the highest salary in baseball and he was hitting .220, he would be unhappy. And if he was getting the lowest salary in baseball and batting .400, he'd be very happy. That's the way I feel about doing this job. Money is a by-product of doing something I like doing extremely well."

(Berkshire Hathaway Annual Meeting, Omaha 1998)

Life Principles

BUFFET ON THE "CLAIM CHECKS" OF LIFE . . .

"I don't have a problem with guilt about money. The way I see it is that my money represents an enormous number of claim checks on society. It's like I have these little pieces of paper that I can turn into consumption. If I wanted to, I could hire 10,000 people to do nothing but paint my picture every day for the rest of my life. And the GNP would go up. But the utility of the product would be zilch, and I would be keeping those 10,000 people from doing AIDS research, or teaching, or nursing. I don't do that, though. I don't use very many of those claim checks. There's nothing material I want very much. And I'm going to give virtually all of those claim checks to charity when my wife and I die."

("Warren Buffett—The Pragmatist," Esquire, *June 1998, p. 59*)

WHAT KIND OF CLIENT DO YOU WANT?

Smart and experienced brokers/advisors have learned that you must be selective about the types of clients you want to attract. If you take any client who comes, you end up with a book of business that can run your life and ruin your life. The way you advertise, publicize, and communicate sends very clear messages about the clients you wish to attract.

Berkshire's high share price is just one of the ways Buffett has chosen to send the message that he wants serious investors who have acquired their shares for the long term. On attracting the right type of clients, this Buffet quote is appropriate:

We could stick a sign outside this hall tonight and put "rock concert" on it, and we'd have one kind of crowd come in. And we could put "ballet" and we'd have a somewhat different kind of crowd come in. Both crowds are fine. But it's a terrible mistake to put rock concert out there if you're going to have a ballet, or vice versa. And the only way I have of sticking a sign on Berkshire, as to the kind of place I'm asking people to enter, is through the communications and policies. (Berkshire Hathaway Annual Meeting, Omaha, 1988)

You need to communicate in a way that reveals your principles regarding long-term investing. Those principles will become a magnet for the type of clients you desire.

13

Let Me Tell You a Story: Storyselling Illustrations, Analogies, and Metaphors

You cannot speak of an ocean to a well-frog, a creature of a narrower sphere.
You cannot speak of ice to a summer insect, the creature of a season.

CHUANG TZU

While the purpose of this chapter is to help you move away from charts and statistics, occasionally we meet a broker who has found a way to simplify charts for clients. Such is the case with storyseller Kay Shirley, who uses the following chart of returns and rates for stocks, bonds, T-bills, and inflation for the years 1926–1998 (Figure 13.1). She emphasizes two points in this chart:

1. Inflation: Kay directs her clients' attention to the far right column, the consumer price index, to demonstrate that in 63 of 73 years we have had inflation, and *we have had inflation for 44 consecutive years!* She also points out that we are going backward if we don't realize at least 3 percent in income, as that is the inflation average for the last 73 years.
2. Stock market recovery: Kay shows her clients that the market dropped 67 percent from 1929 to 1931 and took seven years from the time it dropped to recover. The market dropped 40 percent from 1973 to 1974 and took four years from the time it dropped to recover. She then directs the clients' attention to the 73-year totals at the top of the page that shows common stocks averaging 11.2 percent in spite of these ups and downs compared with 6 percent in bonds and other investments.

FIGURE 13.1 Stocks, Bonds, Treasury Bills, and Inflation

For the 73-year period 1926–1998, compound annual returns, with all income reinvested, have been as follows:

Consumer Price Index	3.2%	Government Bonds	5.7
Treasury Bills	3.8	Corporate Bonds	6.1
		Common Stocks	11.2

ANNUAL PERCENTAGE RETURN INCLUDING INCOME

Year	S&P 500	Corp. Bonds	Gov't Bonds	T-Bills	Consumers Price Index
1926	11.5	7.4	7.8	3.3	−1.5
1927	37.5	7.4	8.9	3.1	−2.1
1928	43.6	2.8	0.1	3.6	−1.0
1929	−8.4	3.3	3.4	4.8	0.2
1930	−24.9	8.0	4.7	2.4	−6.0
1931	−43.3	−1.9	−5.3	1.1	−9.5
1932	−8.2	10.8	16.9	1.0	−10.3
1933	54.0	10.4	−0.1	0.3	0.5
1934	−1.4	13.8	10.0	0.2	2.0
1935	47.7	9.6	5.0	0.2	3.0
1936	33.9	6.7	7.5	0.2	1.2
1937	−35.0	2.8	0.2	0.3	3.1
1938	31.1	6.1	5.5	0.0	−2.6
1939	−0.4	4.0	6.0	0.0	−0.5
1940	−9.8	3.4	6.1	0.0	1.0
1941	−11.6	2.7	0.9	0.1	9.7
1942	20.3	2.6	3.2	0.3	9.3
1943	25.9	2.8	2.1	0.4	3.2
1944	19.8	4.7	2.6	0.3	2.1
1945	38.4	4.1	10.7	0.3	2.3
1946	−8.1	1.7	−0.1	0.4	18.2
1947	5.7	−−2.3	−2.5	0.5	9.0
1948	5.5	4.1	3.4	0.8	2.7
1949	18.8	3.3	6.5	1.1	−1.8
1950	31.7	2.1	0.1	1.2	5.5
1951	24.0	−2.7	−3.9	1.5	5.9
1952	18.4	3.5	1.2	1.7	0.9
1953	−1.0	3.4	3.6	1.6	0.6
1954	52.6	5.4	7.2	0.8	−0.5
1955	31.6	0.5	−1.3	1.6	0.4
1956	6.6	−6.8	−5.6	2.5	2.9
1957	−10.8	8.7	7.5	3.1	3.0
1958	43.4	−2.2	−6.1	1.5	1.6
1959	12.0	−1.0	−2.3	3.0	1.5
1960	0.5	9.1	13.6	2.7	1.5

Year	S&P 500	Corp. Bonds	Gov't Bonds	T-Bills	Consumers Price Index
1961	26.9	4.8	1.0	2.1	0.7
1962	−8.7	8.0	6.9	2.7	1.2
1963	22.8	2.2	1.2	3.1	1.7
1964	16.5	4.8	3.5	3.5	1.2
1965	12.5	−0.5	0.7	3.9	1.9
1966	−10.1	0.2	3.7	4.6	3.4
1967	24.0	−5.0	−9.2	4.2	3.0
1968	11.1	2.6	−0.3	5.2	4.7
1969	−8.5	−8.1	−5.1	6.6	6.1
1970	4.0	18.4	12.1	6.5	5.5
1971	14.3	11.0	13.2	4.4	3.4
1972	19.0	7.3	5.7	3.8	3.4
1973	−14.7	1.1	−1.1	6.9	8.5
1974	−26.5	−3.1	4.4	8.0	12.2
1975	37.2	14.6	9.2	5.8	7.0
1976	23.8	18.7	16.8	5.1	4.8
1977	−7.2	1.7	−0.7	5.1	5.8
1978	6.6	−0.1	−1.2	7.2	9.0
1979	18.4	−4.2	−1.2	10.4	13.3
1980	32.4	−2.8	−4.0	11.2	12.4
1981	−4.9	−1.2	1.9	14.7	8.9
1982	21.4	42.6	40.4	10.5	3.9
1983	27.5	8.3	0.7	8.8	3.8
1984	6.3	15.9	15.5	9.9	4.0
1985	32.2	30.1	31.0	7.7	3.8
1986	15.6	19.9	24.5	6.2	1.1
1987	5.2	−0.3	−2.7	5.5	4.4
1988	15.8	10.7	9.7	6.4	4.4
1989	31.5	16.2	18.1	8.4	4.7
1990	−3.2	6.6	8.2	7.8	6.1
1991	30.5	19.9	19.3	5.6	3.1
1992	7.7	9.4	8.1	3.6	2.9
1993	10.0	13.2	18.2	2.9	2.8
1994	1.3	−5.8	−7.8	3.9	2.7
1995	37.4	27.2	31.7	5.6	2.5
1996	23.1	1.4	−0.9	5.2	3.3
1997	33.4	13.0	15.9	5.3	1.7
1998	25.7	8.6	15.5	4.8	1.7

Sources: Ibbotson Assoc., Standard & Poor's Salomon Brothers, Sherson Lehman Brothers, Merrill Lynch, U.S. Bureau of Labor Statistics

ILLUSTRATIONS AND METAPHORS

Following are illustrations and metaphors that we have gathered from brokers and advisors across America. These people have shared their ideas in hope that others will use them and find the same level of success they have already experienced. The illustrations cover a variety of investment themes, such as diversification, investing for the long term, growth and value, risk tolerance, and so on.

Pick out illustrations that you prefer and begin to use them in your client presentations. See for yourself what a difference illustrative and imaginative speech can make. Storyselling really works!

If you have an illustration, anecdote, or metaphor you'd like to share or if you'd like to see updated examples, visit our Web site at www.storysellers.com.

Annuities

ON ANNUITIES AND THE DESTRUCTIVE POWER OF TAXATION

"**The long-term goal** of investing is to multiply the eggs in our basket. Most people are very focused on producing more eggs (getting high returns) but pay little attention to the fox that perpetually robs the hen house. If you ignore the fox, soon there will be nothing left to produce more eggs. That fox is taxation. The annuity I'm about to show you builds a high fence around the hen house and keeps the foxes out, allowing your eggs to multiply."

Annuities

ON SELLING
SELECTED ANNUITIES

"A broker has a Russian doll set on her desk. When introducing an annuity with diverse investment options, she places the doll set in front of the client and says, 'The annuity we're talking about is very much like this Russian doll set. On the surface it looks like one investment, but in fact (she starts pulling dolls out) it is many investment options rolled into one. If you want mutual funds, they're in the annuity. If you want a guaranteed rate of return on some or all of your money, it is in the annuity. In fact, this particular annuity has X options for you to choose from, all in a tax-sheltered investment vehicle.'"

Inflation

ON INFLATION

"A simple way to see the effects of inflation is to look at postage stamps and the bills you attach them to. In 1983, it cost you 20¢ to mail in your monthly payment. In 1999, it costs you 33¢. The increase in postage alone is 60 percent. Add to that how much more you are now sending to the electric company, the cable company, and so on, and you see the effects of inflation. What will these things cost in the year 2013? Certainly much more than they do today. This issue is all the more pressing if you plan on retiring. As Roman statesman Cato the Elder said, "Cessation of work is not accompanied by cessation of expenses."

(Roger Thomas)

ON OUTLIVING
YOUR INCOME

"One fellow said that he thought the perfect retirement plan would be one where the only check that bounced was the one written to his undertaker.

Unfortunately, most of us have no idea how long either we (or our money) are going to live. People live longer today. If you're 62 today, there's a good chance you'll be around 23 more years. We need to make sure your money is around as long as you are. Your job is to keep yourself going—and my job is to help you keep your money going."

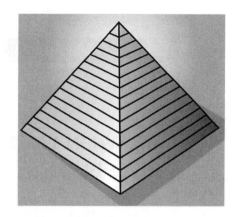

BUILDING A PYRAMID FOR YOUR ASSETS

"Building a solid portfolio is very much like building the pyramids of long ago. Ancient Egyptians built pyramids for *keeping the family treasures,* and these pyramids were designed to *stand the test of time.* That's why we're going to look at an asset allocation plan that has stood the test of time. The asset groups I show you today have returned an average of 15 percent over a 20-year period. I think your family treasures need the same sort of care and protection that pyramids provided in ancient times. Here's how we'll build your pyramid . . ."

Investing for the Long Run

ON WHEN TO START INVESTING

"**An older man** wanted to plant a certain type of tree. A young gardener told the man that this particular tree would take 40 years to blossom. The older man replied, 'Then, we'd better start this afternoon.'"

Investing for the Long Run

ON THE URGENCY
OF INVESTING NOW

"A certain advisor has a drawer full of 72-inch measuring tapes. He asks his client, 'At what age do you want to retire?'
Client replies, 'At age 65.'
The advisor then pulls out a measuring tape and a scissors and cuts the tape at 65 inches and lets the tape roll out to the floor. He then asks, 'How old are you today?'
The client replies, '51 years old.'
The advisor then cuts the tape at 51 inches, lets the large part of the tape fall to the floor, and holds the 14 inches from 51 to 65 inches. Pointing to the tape on the floor, he says, 'That's done and over. This *(pointing to tape in his hand)* is what we have to work with. We have some serious investment work to do from now until 65 *(hands 14-inch tape to customer)*. You can keep this as a reminder."

(Don Connelly)

ON THE URGENCY OF INVESTING NOW

"After calculating the amount his client will need to retire, a broker asks his clients: 'At what age do you want to retire?'
    Client replies, '65.'
    Broker asks, 'How old are you now?'
    Client: '45.'
    Broker: 'How much do you make a year?'
    Client: '$50,000.'
    Broker: 'OK, if my math is correct, you have 240 monthly paychecks left in your working career. According to our previous discussion you need $500,000 to draw from at retirement. Today you have $140,000. We're $360,000 shy right now. What is the likelihood that you will have saved $1,500 toward retirement out of each of your last 240 checks?'
    Client, 'Not likely.'
    Broker: 'Then, here is the plan we'll need to follow to get you there . . .'
    (Broker then gives an illustration of investments and rate of return to reach retirement goal.)"

Investing for the Long Run

ON MARKET UPS
AND DOWNS

"Do you know what investing for the long run but listening to market news every day is like? It's like a man walking up a big hill with a yo-yo and keeping his eyes fixed on the yo-yo instead of the hill."

(Alan Abelson)

ON PREDICTING BEAR MARKETS AND LONG-TERM INVESTING

"Predicting when we will see a bear market is equal to predicting when a dart will hit a bull's-eye. The majority of the time throughout market history, the markets have been rising. History shows that the chances of your money growing in stocks is much like the odds of your next dart hitting any number on the dartboard but a bull's-eye. If you are going to try to time moving money in and out of the market, you have to ask yourself how confident you can hit a bull's-eye every time you do it."

Investing for the Long Run

ON PATIENCE IN INVESTING

"In the past I've met many investors who did not understand the 'seasonality' of their investments. Every portfolio will go through cycles or seasons. There will be times when new buds of opportunity will appear. There will be times of prodigious growth. There will be times when we harvest from that growth. And, quite frankly, there will be times when the tree will look barren in its winter season.

I've seen too many people who want to uproot their tree in the middle of winter. These people never prosper. With just a little patience they would have seen the season change and new growth appear. These things are all cyclical.

I view your portfolio as a valuable growing tree. My job is to know when to water it (buy new investments), when to harvest it (sell), when to fertilize it (buy), *and* when to prune (sell). With patience and care we know it will grow strong and fruitful."

INVESTING FOR THE LONG RUN

"Imagine that you had to drive from New York City to Los Angeles. You're in downtown Manhattan hopelessly stuck in traffic. Bicycle messengers are whizzing past. You jump out of your car, sell your car on the spot (at a ridiculously low price), buy a bicycle, and continue your trip to the West Coast.

As absurd as this scenario sounds, investors do it everyday when they make short-term decisions for long-term journeys. Stick with a vehicle that will take you to the end of the road."

(Don Connelly)

Investing for the Long Run

ON MEASURING YOUR PROGRESS

"One broker likes to ask his clients if they are planning a trip in their car in the near future. He then asks, 'Would you mind doing me a favor and measuring how far it is from here to there—but rather than measuring by your odometer, I'd like you to use this' (he hands them a 12-inch ruler). 'You see, Mr. and Mrs. Client, as ridiculous as it sounds to use a 12-inch ruler to measure a long journey, this is what people do every day with their investment journey. They read mutual fund prices in the paper every day, they watch CNBC, and worry. They are measuring their journey in inches instead of miles. I don't want you to make that mistake.'"

Investing for the Long Run

ON THE IRRATIONAL MARKETPLACE

"We are in the only business in the world where shoppers act extremely illogically. When prices are rising people, get into an emotional heat and buy all they can. When stocks and funds go on sale, people stay away in droves and, worse, sell what they bought high at rummage sale prices."

Investing for the Long Run

STAYING THE COURSE ILLUSTRATION OF FINANCIAL HEADLINES

"Are you following investment wisdom or financial headlines?

One financial magazine listed 50 funds in five years that were great, best, most dependable, or number one. However, none of the lists contained the same funds. The fund that named the best this year wasn't on the lists the four previous years. So what are we to do? Change funds every year?

Here are some headlines you'll never see in a financial magazine:

- Time in the market is more important than timing of the market.
- Don't invest until you have clearly defined goals.
- Investors with trusted financial advisors outperform do-it-yourselfers over meaningful time horizons."

(Roger Thomas)

Investing for the Long Run

STAYING THE COURSE HOW IMPORTANT IS THE DOW JONES INDUSTRIAL AVERAGE?

"People often become anxious and fearful when they hear the media shouting about the Dow going up and down. Have you ever wondered how important the number really is?

The Dow Jones Industrial Average represents only 30 stocks out of the more than 35,000 stocks that trade on the various exchanges in America. The Dow represents only .0007 percent of all the stocks traded. The number the media shouts about excludes what is happening to the other .9993 percent of stocks.

Even when the Dow is going down or on its weekly roller-coaster, there is good investment opportunity in the other .9993 percent of stocks out there. Don't let the headlines about the Dow average seem any more significant than they are. It's like saying that the NFL is in a major slump because one running back is having a bad year."

(Roger Thomas)

Investment Principles

HOW THE MARKET PRICES STOCKS

"It has been said that the market is a barometer, not a thermometer. What does that mean? It means the price of the stock today is not established by 'taking the temperature' of that company today but by anticipating what the temperature of that company will be tomorrow. The market looks at 'barometric pressures' on the company and tries to anticipate how they will affect the temperature a month from now and a year from now.

Wall Street, in many ways, acts like the weatherman. Our opportunities for gain come from being able to recognize when the weatherman is wrong about a certain company."

Investment Principles

FOR THOSE WHO WORRY ABOUT CHANGES

"**The U.S. standard-gauge** railroad track is four feet, eight-and-a-half inches wide. Why such an odd measure? Because that was the width in England and the United States when railroads were built by British expatriates.

Where did the English get that measure? The first rail lines were built by the same people who built the tramways that preceded railroads. They built the trams with the same jigs and tools used for building wagons. The wagons were built to that width so their wheels would fit the ruts of England's ancient long-distance roads.

The ruts had been made by the war chariots brought to England by the occupying Imperial Roman army. And the chariots were that wide to accommodate the rear ends of two horses. You're not alone if you struggle with change."

(Don Connelly)

Irrational Investors

CHASING THE HOT FUND

"Have you ever been sitting in traffic in a lane that's not moving and watching people switch to the lane next to you that's empty? You're frustrated by your lack of progress and annoyed by all the people passing you. So you switch lanes. No sooner do you switch lanes when the traffic stops in *that* lane.

This is exactly what happens to investors, who chase this year's hot fund. History shows that those who constantly 'change lanes' to the year's hottest funds don't keep up with the next year's overall average returns."

(Brett Van Bortel)

Irrational Investors

ON STAYING ABOVE
THE EMOTIONAL FRAY

"People become hyper about the markets when they listen to hyperbole. The press, in an effort to get viewers' attention, exaggerate events in the marketplace and thus excite the emotions of investors who are swayed by fear. This emotional Ping-Pong game results in illogical investment behavior, such as buying at market highs and selling at market lows. The wise investor has learned to look past the colorful adjectives that describe daily market fluctuations and to keep his or her eyes fixed on long-term trends."

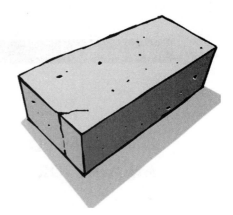

Irrational Investors

HOW TO RESPOND WHEN THE MARKET FALLS

"**A broker who** kept a brick on his desk would tell his new clients, 'One of these days the market will go down and you'll be upset—maybe so upset you'll want to throw this brick through my window. Before you decide to throw this brick through my window I want you to do one thing—I want you to write a check to your mutual fund company and tie it to this brick, because when the market falls, you should be thinking about buying more shares.'"

ON THE NEED FOR AN ADVISOR

"**What if you** were going on a trip and you were offered the opportunity to fly on one of two jet airplanes? The first is piloted by an experienced pilot who is being paid to pilot; the second has no pilot but you are allowed to fly it yourself. If you choose the plane without the pilot, a computer will be installed in the cockpit that hooks you up to an Internet site that will tell you everything you need to know about flying.

Which plane do you want for your journey? What you're paying for when you hire an advisor is not information—you can get that anywhere. You're paying for experience. I've been there in bad weather and know how to make a safe landing."

Why Use an Advisor?

ON THE NEED FOR A BROKER/ADVISOR

"When you travel to a faraway place, don't you like to get the advice of a travel agent who has been there? Why or why not?

If you just look at all the literature and try to map out a course for yourself, you may end up with some very unpleasant surprises when you get there. That's where travel professionals come in. They've been there. They know whom you can believe and whom you can't. They know the real story. What you're paying for with a travel agent is *experience* and *peace of mind.* You don't need any surprises.

You face the same dilemma with your money. All kinds of do-it-yourself brochures and literature are available on Web sites, voice mail systems, and glossy paper. But try talking to someone who has been there and knows the real story—and see where you get.

I act as your investment travel guide and tell you which destinations are worth going to. The difference is between information and wisdom."

WHY YOU NEED AN ADVISOR WHO PAYS ATTENTION TO YOUR PORTFOLIO

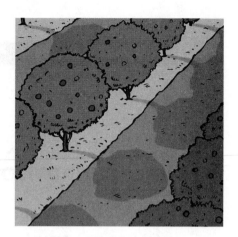

"The amazing thing about this picture is that these two orange groves border one another. They experienced the same amount of rain, cold, wind, and so on, and yet they produced entirely different results.

The only difference between these two groves is ownership. The bountiful grove has a local owner who responded quickly to changing conditions and kept a close eye on his crop. The barren grove's owner lives in New York and would call occasionally to see how things were going. His hired help would tell him things were fine."

Why Use an Advisor?

ON THE NEED FOR AN ADVISOR WHO PAYS ATTENTION

"**Have you ever** planted a seed and forgotten to water it? You know, there's more work to growing beautiful flowers than just dropping a seed in the ground. When the ground's dry, we water it. When it's cold, we protect it.

A lot of advisors will show you a pretty picture of a flower, drop your investment seed in the ground, and then forget about it. Around here we believe it's what we do after we plant the seed that matters. Here's what kind of service and maintenance you can expect from us . . ."

NOTE: At the end of his presentation, a broker we met had the package of flower seeds sitting on his desk and placed it in front of his client and gave this little talk.

FINDING AN ADVISOR YOU TRUST

"**An advisor in** the Midwest once handed a kernel of corn to a farmer client and asked, 'Do you expect me to believe that you could somehow magically produce row upon row, acres upon acres of corn from this little kernel?'

You and I both know you could. There is no questioning the potential of a seed. The real question would be, 'Do I believe in your competence as a farmer to get the job done? Am I willing to trust you with this seed?'

Your money is no different from this seed. It has the same potential. The only question you really need to answer is, 'Do you believe in my competence as an advisor to manage that growth?'"

Why Use an Advisor?

HOW MUCH CAN YOU MAKE IN A DOWN OR FLAT MARKET?

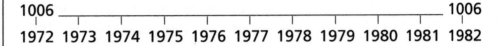

1006 ————————————————————— 1006
1972 1973 1974 1975 1976 1977 1978 1979 1980 1981 1982

On December 26, 1972, and October 26, 1982, the Dow Jones Industrial Average (DJIA) closed at exactly the same level—1,006.

If you had invested $100,000 in 1972, what do you think it would have been worth in 1982? The answer to that question may surprise you. Some think that their $100,000 would still be worth $100,000 because the market didn't rise—but they would be mistaken.

If you had invested $100,000 in the 30 stocks that make up the DJIA, your money would have grown to $169,000 because of dividend reinvestment.

If you had invested your money in a professionally managed mutual fund, your $100,000 would have grown to $221,000. The expertise of these professionals pays off.

But if you had invested with a trusted financial advisor who suggested a diversified portfolio of three time-tested mutual funds, your account would have grown to $240,000.

What difference can a good advisor make? In this ten-year period the answer is about $69,000!

(Roger Thomas)

Why Use an Advisor?

TEN REASONS WHY I INVEST IN NO-LOAD FUNDS

1. I feel secure in putting my hard-earned life savings in a mailbox and sending them to total strangers.
2. I prefer the service I receive from faceless clerks at 800 numbers to a local investment professional.
3. I have plenty of time to read finance journals, investment magazines, and newsletters.
4. I believe publications that depend on advertising revenue from no-load funds can render impartial and objective investment advice.
5. I prefer being thought of as a computer entry rather than a person.
6. I feel fund companies that sell to a mass market care about me and understand my specific financial goals, time horizons, and risk tolerance.
7. I have nerves of steel. The 507-point market decline on October 19, 1987, didn't concern me—neither do bear markets.
8. I can time the market and make fund switches with laser precision.
9. I don't find the 4000+ no-load fund alternatives overwhelming. By reading five prospectuses a day, I'll know them all in about 26 months.
10. I am not willing to pay fees for professional services. In addition to managing my own investment portfolio, I also diagnose and treat my own medical problems, represent myself in legal matters, and file my own taxes.

(Van Kampen Funds, Inc.)

Investment Risks and Returns

ON ASSET ALLOCATION

"Markets are unpredictable. That's why we preach putting your money in many buckets, or diversification. Like the Ferris wheel, if one bucket happens to turn upside down, all the other buckets you've invested in are still upright. What kind of shape would you be in if all your money were in that one bucket? If one bucket goes upside down, you'd better be in the others."

(Don Connelly)

PUT YOUR INVESTMENTS IN A PYRAMID

"There are six asset classes that we will invest in. They are

- midsize growth (17 percent);
- growth and income (13.12 percent);
- large cap (12.99 percent);
- income and growth equity income (11.2 percent);
- high-income bonds (8.72 percent); and
- corporate bonds (8.32 percent).

The number they have returned is the average annualized return over 20 years. We have not considered any asset class that does not have a 20-year track record. With this balanced approach, you would have averaged a 15 percent return over a 20-year period. That means if you're starting today with $50,000, in 20 years you will have X."

(Lowell Jackson)

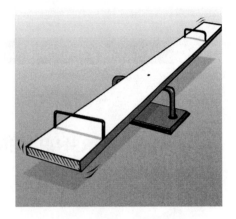

Investment Risks and Returns

ON BONDS AND INTEREST RATES

(You can use a pencil for this illustration) "The relationship between interest rates and bond prices is just like a see-saw. If interest rates are up *[turn pencil]*, then bond prices fall. If interest rates are down, then bond prices will rise *[turn pencil]*."

LOANERSHIP VERSUS OWNERSHIP

Would you rather be an owner of a company or a loaner to a company? When the company prospers, who stands to prosper the most? The owners or the bankers? The owners will pay the bankers (loaners) only what they have to, but they'll pay themselves with the rest of the profits.

Loanership versus ownership is the easiest way to separate your investment choices.

LOANERSHIP	OWNERSHIP
Certificates of Deposit	Common Stock
Corporate Bonds	Mutual Funds
Municipal Bonds	
Government Bonds	

Loanership versus Ownership Returns

Ten-Year Investment Returns

The following figures show the best returns with loanership vehicles and only a median performance with a mutual fund.

- Municipal bond: $10,000 invested grew to $20,598
- Corporate bond: $10,000 invested grew to $23,481
- Government bond: $10,000 invested grew to $24,212
- Certificate of deposit: $10,000 invested grew to $26,599
- Growth & income mutual fund: $10,000 invested grew to $30,409

(Roger Thomas)

Investment Risks and Returns

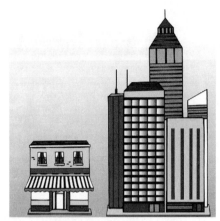

ON WHY WE BUY MUTUAL FUNDS

"I'd like you to look at this picture and I'll ask you a question, 'What are the chances of the business on the left going broke?' Pretty fair chance, right? Now, let me ask you this, "What are the odds of every business in that skyline going broke?' Extremely remote. That's why we invest in mutual funds, because owning many companies is much safer than owning just one company."

Investment Risks and Returns

DEFINING GROWTH
AND VALUE

"Many growth investors are willing to pay a high price for fear that the price will be higher in the future. The uncertainty the growth investor must live with is, 'How much can you inflate this ball before it bursts?'

Value investors are willing to pay a discounted price for a ball that has lost some air on hopes that market and management changes will again inflate the ball and once again raise its value. An uncertainty the value investor must live with: "What if the ball loses more air and falls even further?"

Investment Risks and Returns

ON TAKING UNNECESSARY RISKS

"**A lot of** investment opportunities that people get all excited about remind me of the 'Sunday pin placement' in a major golf tournament. Often in golf tournaments and Sunday golf games, the pin is purposely put in a place to tempt you to take a risk that could either reward you richly (if you hit a perfect shot) or ruin your chances for a win (if you don't).

It's easy to think we can go for it, but most golfers, even the most skilled, end up in some sort of trouble when they do. It's better to play to the middle of the green and take moderate risks with a less dramatic downside."

Investment Risks and Returns

ILLUSTRATION: THE RISK-RETURN RAILROAD

"Risk and return operate like railroad tracks. They run exactly parallel to one another. Anything that promises great return with little risk is sure to derail you. No matter how high or low the desired return, the level of risk runs parallel with it. If you want low risk and an even ride with few ups and downs, then you choose the track that will get you that. If you want higher returns, you must ride a rail with steeper ups and downs. The question you must ask yourself: 'What kind of journey do I want?'"

Investment Risks and Returns

STOCK VALUE VERSUS YIELD

"**What do you** tell retirees who are receiving monthly income from the investments but are worried about the fluctuations in the value of the investments? One advisor used the following illustration:

If you owned farmland, what would you be most concerned about, your yearly yield or fluctuations in the value of your land? Farmers are most concerned about getting paid each year for their crops and are not worrying about land values, which move up and down.

That's the way it is with your investments. Even though some of the underlying investments may move up and down, your number one concern is to make sure that you get your check every month."

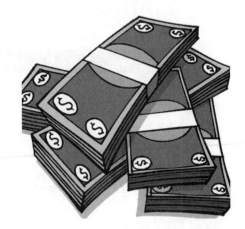

Life Principles

HOW MUCH MONEY IS A BILLION DOLLARS?

Broker Art Rose likes to share this illustration with his clients. "It seems that every day we read about a company being bought or sold for X billion dollars. Have you ever stopped to consider how much money a billion dollars is? Ponder this: if you were to spend a $1,000 a day every day from the time Jesus was born until today, you still would not have spent a billion dollars."

Index